RAISING NONVIOLENT CHILDREN
IN A VIOLENT WORLD

A FAMILY HANDBOOK

RAISING NONVIOLENT CHILDREN
IN A VIOLENT WORLD

DR. MICHAEL OBSATZ

Augsburg
MINNEAPOLIS

RAISING NONVIOLENT CHILDREN IN A VIOLENT WORLD
A Family Handbook

Cover photo from PhotoDisc
Cover design by David Meyer
Book design by Elizabeth Boyce

ISBN 0-8066-3700-5

The paper used in this publication meets the minimum requirements of American National Standard for Information Sciences—Permanence of Paper for Printed Library Materials, ANSI Z329.48-1984

Manufactured in the U.S.A.   AF 9-3700

02   01   00   99   98   1   2   3   4   5   6   7   8   9   10

CONTENTS

ACKNOWLEDGMENTS

I wish to thank my dear wife, Nancy, for her ideas, support, and encouragement during the writing of this book.

I would like to dedicate this book to my three creative children, Sharyn, Kevin, and Molly, who lead productive and nonviolent lives.

Special thanks to my friends Herb Laube, Stan Shapiro, Peter Remes, Ellen Houghton, Kent Johnson, Laura Lucas-Silvis, Art Decker, and Dave Decker, who have nurtured me. I am also grateful for the Butters and Cunningham families who read a draft of the book and commented, and for my editor, Ronald Klug, who provided insights, encouragement, and resources.

INTRODUCTION: RAISING NONVIOLENT CHILDREN IN A VIOLENT WORLD

As we approach the twenty-first century, we face a choice. We can begin to control violent behavior, both on a national and international level, or we can continue to let it control and perhaps destroy us. We have enough knowledge to be able to significantly decrease violence. . . . Our country was not created so that future generations could maximize profit at any cost. It was created with humanistic, egalitarian, altruistic goals. We must put our enormous resources and talents to the task of creating a children's culture that is consistent with these goals.

—Myriam Miedzian

I n my "Raising Nonviolent Children in a Violent World" workshops, I am often approached by parents who are fearful about violence. They are afraid that their children will suffer a violent attack by another child, a group of children, an adult, or a group of adults. They worry about violent behavior they observe in their own children, whether in group play or in interaction between siblings. They see their child aggressively pulling something out of another child's hands or making hostile and degrading comments.

Bullying is said to be a fact of life among children. From a very young age, children learn that they are on the bottom of the barrel when it comes to power, and some respond with a need to dominate and control others. Others become fearful, shy, or prone to the aggressive hostility of others. Some children are the perpetrators, and some are the victims.

Violence is all around us. Network news informs us of one crime after another. Wars are being waged all over the world. Children become immersed in television violence. One blockbuster movie after another comes out with volcanoes, tornados, earthquakes—and murders, robberies, rapes, gang wars, underworld crime, and explosions.

In toy stores, children can buy toys of destruction, action figures with guns, wrestlers, boxers, soldiers, and superheroes with enormous muscles and weapons. Television cartoons are filled with squashing and pulverizing, harassment, name calling, bullying, and ridicule. Program after program aimed at children finds humor in putdowns, shaming, and critical remarks.

While some people accept violence as a necessary part of life, others decry the pervasiveness of it. Some claim that children need to act out their fears and fantasies through fairy tales. But when children are exposed to continuous violence in the media, they begin to "normalize" it. They do not learn nonviolent methods of coping with stress, conflict, and power.

What Makes Our Society So Violent?

The United States was born of violence. The American Revolution involved the killing of many British and American soldiers. In the course of settling the West, many Native Americans were killed. As the nation developed industrially, it became a superpower, destined to protect the world. Affluence was achieved through intense competition and aggressive behavior. Clearly the United States is not the first culture to be violent nor will it be the last. But at times, it seems as if America is obsessed with power, with winning at all costs. Still in its adolescence, perhaps our relatively new country has a sense of rebellion in its bones.

Our educational system seems to reinforce individualism more than collaboration. Our economic system rewards the accumulation of wealth and the outdoing of the competition. In more recent years, the gap has widened between the haves and have-nots. There are more people below the poverty line, and because media representations show poor children how the other half lives, this discrepancy is more acutely felt.

We are also teaching young people to want immediate gratification. More people seem to be impulsive and unable to handle even the smallest frustrations. Terminated employees have been known to shoot up their former places of employment. Stressed-out drivers aggressively hurt others on the highways in road rage. As the pace of life intensifies and the gap between ideals and reality grows larger, people vent their frustration with anger, rage, and violent behavior. Even some small towns that used to feel safe are now threatened with child abductions.

It may also be that we are becoming more aware of violence that has always existed. There are more reports of rape and child abuse. As shelters emerge for battered women, more battered women are coming forward. We may be more aware, more concerned, and more determined to put a stop to violence.

What Is Violence?

There are at least six kinds of violence:
1. violence toward the environment, which involves overconsumption, littering, polluting, and disregarding nature
2. physical or sexual violence toward others, which includes hitting, punching, kicking, raping, domestic violence, and sexual abuse

3. verbal and emotional violence toward others—for example, ridicule, verbal harassment, shaming, name calling, and teasing
4. violence toward the self, such as starving oneself, binging and purging, and physically abusing oneself
5. passive violence toward others, which includes shunning and ostracizing them
6. cultural violence—the creation of destructive products and violent role models by those in power positions and the use of violence to sell products without considering its effects on others

Where Does Violence Come From?

We all have tendencies to be violent. If frustrated or pushed beyond our limits, any of us might engage in aggressive and violent behavior. Violence appears to come from feelings of loneliness, powerlessness, and low self-esteem, from the frustration and rage of not being loved for one's very being. Violent responses come when individuals' needs for love, nurturing, support, caring, and validation are not met. Violence may result when people lack the knowledge of nonviolent ways to cope with life's issues, problems, and difficulties. Violence also can become a lifestyle, a normalized way of living and acting.

Dr. David Walsh, author of *Selling Out America's Children,* believes that when children ages three to ten watch excessive hours of violence in the media, the limbic system of their brains is stimulated by sex, violence, and humor. The cortex, responsible for abstract thinking, conceptual ability, and empathy, does not develop adequately. As a result, some children lack the capacity for empathic thinking or understanding the point of view of another. When this is lacking, children do not develop a conscience. They do not understand how others feel and take no responsibility for the effects of their behavior on others.

Violent behavior and feelings seem to be the symptoms of a society in emotional pain and one hungering for spiritual connectedness. People who are not loved and nurtured do not have the energy or resources to give love to others. Children lacking this support and nurturing hurt inside and often vent this pain through anger at others. Children who lack parental understanding and teaching don't develop the skills to solve life's problems through such nonviolent means as negotiating, compromising, clarifying, and collaborating.

Children can be helped to process the violent messages they receive from media. They can be taught that violence is not an appropriate solution to life's problems. They are certainly capable of learning how to foresee when a situation might turn violent, and they can understand that it is often courageous to walk away from violent confrontations. They need to learn these nonviolent alternatives from healthy, adult role models.

How Can America Become More Peace Loving?

Violence in America may be a by-product of a culture losing sight of its commitment to community, altruism, and compassion. A culture that values each and every living human being can demonstrate this by

1. making children a high priority
2. valuing people for their inherent worth rather than for material wealth and social status
3. taking care of those who are poor in spirit and material goods
4. making morality and ethical decision making vitally important
5. supporting victims who experience abuse
6. teaching children that helping others is gratifying
7. encouraging independence but also encouraging community building

8. supporting a work ethic by which all workers have dignity
9. valuing peacemakers and teaching peaceful conflict resolution
10. appreciating ordinary heroes

What Roles Do Parents Play?

Parents who are oriented to peace and spirituality can encourage their children to love others, share what they have, and value other people's needs and feelings. Parents who are proactive in their child rearing can equip their children to cope with the strong cultural machine that tends to focus on materialistic and self-centered values. Children are capable of learning all the necessary skills and attitudes that promote nonviolence and peaceful solutions to problems and conflicts.

Healthy adulthood means having a sense of financial responsibility. Mature adults spend within their means and manage their money well. On the interpersonal level, healthy adults keep their commitments to others, develop and maintain nurturing and supportive friendships, and respect the rights of others. They know the difference between sexual and nonsexual touch. They respect the boundaries of others. Adults who act maturely take responsibility for raising their own children. They are able to negotiate and compromise. They can be cooperative as well as competitive.

While mature adults have an awareness of their own needs, wants, and goals, they are not obsessed with getting everything all the time. They reach out to others, helping in the community, and offering support where they can. They mentor others and become good role models. They live a life of balance with respect to work and play, rest and exercise, alone time and social time. Mature and healthy adults are problem solvers. They can see alternative solutions.

On a spiritual level, they know when to control and when to let go. They have developed their own sense of personal spirituality, which may or may not involve institutional religion. Most of the time, however, they belong to some type of faith community. They acknowledge their losses and can grieve them. They don't hold onto grudges. They forgive and move on. They develop a sense of purpose or mission that gives them direction and priorities, and they can accept their limits and mistakes and forgive themselves.

Healthy adults celebrate successes and milestones and create meaningful traditions and rituals. They live effectively in the present while planning for the future. We can all teach our children to become peace-loving adults. The twenty-one skills listed here can help parents equip their children to cope with a changing world in nonviolent ways.

The first group of skills are *personal growth skills*. The group includes
1. setting goals and planning for your future
2. disciplining yourself, improving your skills
3. brainstorming and problem solving
4. coping with disappointments by grieving, forgiving, and bouncing back
5. asking for nurturing and care when you need it

The second group involves *self-defense skills*. It includes
6. protecting your rights and privacy
7. avoiding potentially violent people
8. disarming the bully
9. using media wisely
10. creating safer schools and neighborhoods

The third group lists *interpersonal skills*—the ones that deal with how to relate effectively with others. It includes
11. identifying feelings and empathizing with others

12. respecting other people's rights
13. choosing good friends
14. expressing ideas and listening to others
15. collaborating and sharing ideas
16. compromising and negotiating
17. controlling impulses to strike out
18. venting anger nonviolently
19. nurturing and caring for others
20. supporting others through losses and disappointments
21. learning to play nonviolently

Finally, ideas are presented about creating nonviolent spiritual families.

How to Use This Workbook

This workbook is designed to help parents teach children those skills that will lead to productivity, adult maturity, and a nonviolent society. Set aside a period of time to use this workbook. You may choose one or two specific evenings a week. Twice a week might be a good amount of time, but of course it depends upon parental commitments and children's free time. It would be helpful to have an hour set aside for parents to read the chapter first.

In a two-parent family, either one or both parents can work on this book with the children. If a child is old enough to read and comprehend the material, he or she can read it after you have. If a child is under eight, you can explain the various parts of each chapter to him or her. If you have children of different ages, you might want to group them for the discussions but spend individual time with them going through the chapters and the exercises. Each chapter has "A Word for Children" specifically aimed at their reading and vocabulary level.

After reading a chapter to your child (if he or she is too young to read) or reading it together (if he or she is older), you might ask what he or she thought were the most important points in the chapter and why. Then you can work through the exercises together. Write or think about your answers and then discuss them. Reread any parts of the chapter that you find especially interesting or relevant to your particular situation. You may work on the chapters in order or select the ones that seem most interesting to you or to your children.

You might also choose to work on this book in a group setting, such as a parent support group in a church or an adult education program. Parents might meet alone for forty-five minutes to read and discuss each chapter while their children are involved in some other activity. The adults can discuss some of the complexities of teaching the personal growth, self-defense, and interpersonal skills. Parents can then work individually with their children at home or in the group setting. Again certain chapters can be selected by the parents as most important.

Once children master the skills in this book, they can become mentors and tutors for other children. Older children can model and teach these skills to younger children. Parents and teachers can help children develop skits and monologues that demonstrate the use of these skills. These skills can also be the basis for a play written by parents, teachers, and children that can be performed in a school or church setting. This workbook might also be used as part of a school curriculum, with teachers collaborating to create additional hands-on exercises.

Raising nonviolent children in today's world is a challenge. The benefits and joys that both parent and child receive from learning peacemaking skills far outweigh the energy and time it takes. With determination, faith, commitment, and God's help, parents can lead children into a more peace-loving twenty-first century. Are you ready to begin this exciting and gratifying journey?

PERSONAL GROWTH SKILLS

1

SETTING GOALS AND PLANNING FOR YOUR FUTURE

Several terms give an accurate feeling for the nature of an ideal. "Life direction" and "purpose" are two of them. Although some people are more immediately aware of this fact than others, we all live our lives with some kind of motivation, which creates a direction of personal development and a sense of purpose in living. For one person, it may be striving for fame; for a second, healing the suffering of humanity; yet for a third, it might be creative expression.

—Mark Thurston

When children and adults develop a sense of purpose, their lives have a focus. People who set personally meaningful goals are less likely to be violent because they put their energy into planning for their future. They are less impulsive and less likely to do something that will harm their chances for future success.

One of the greatest problems facing American society today is that its adults and youth lack a sense of purpose. Many people have not thought about what they really want to become. They go along, day by day, and merely get by. They lack clear goals and priorities. They drift in and out of jobs and relationships. They have no clear picture of spirituality in their lives. Most violent people probably have no constructive life plan and no productive life goals.

Children can learn how to set goals for themselves—goals about health, career, lifestyle, spiritual growth, intellectual and emotional maturity, and relationships. It is vital that parents share with their children their own goals and plans for achieving such. Children learn by example and can tell that their parents are purposeful people who reap joys and benefits from having dreams, goals, and plans. Stephen Covey, in *The Seven Habits of Highly Effective People,* claims that you have to "begin with the end in mind." Where and how you begin is determined by what you see for yourself in the future.

What are the areas in which goals need to be set? There are two categories of goals: those set for oneself and those that include the larger community. Personal goals involve physical health and well-being, relationships, spiritual growth, emotional maturity, career or vocation, and intellectual goals. Community goals involve those things that the individual strives for that will bring about change in the community—such as creating low income housing or feeding the hungry.

In the personal area of physical health and well-being, children can work toward developing healthy nutritional habits and can learn how to balance rest, work, exercise, and eating. Children can also set goals to develop their athletic capabilities. They can set up strategies to practice and improve specific physical skills.

In the area of spiritual growth, parents can help children formulate goals related to learning about God, becoming closer to God, and living a spiritually focused life. Strategies for achieving these goals might include reading the Bible, regular prayer time, church or synagogue attendance, going to Sunday school, and participating in spiritual community activities, retreats, and events.

In the area of relationships, children can set goals in developing strong friendships that involve nurturing and support. They can be asked to list the qualities they desire in a friendship and then can work on developing those qualities in themselves.

With respect to career goals, children as young as ten can begin to explore possible career choices. They might interview people from different career backgrounds and shadow them for a few days. In this way, they can see what it actually feels like to be a doctor, reporter, day-care provider, teacher, or architect.

For intellectual goals, children may decide to read a dozen books, practice their writing skills, or learn to read faster. They might set a goal to write two poems a week or learn more about insects or history.

For emotional maturity, children can set goals about gaining self-esteem and controlling their temper. Parents can help children by brainstorming with them some goals for handling problems calmly without getting too angry or anxious.

Community goals include helping prepare food for a homeless shelter, raking leaves for an elderly neighbor, providing hot meals for shut-ins, or visiting elderly people in a nursing home.

Once children establish goals for their lives, they can work to develop a plan of action. How will they get there? If one wishes to become a minister, for example, one has to do well in high school, get good grades, go to college, and then attend seminary. A child who has this goal in mind begins by focusing on his or her learning and planning very carefully how each step can lead to the next. Developing a life plan involves seeing how each part of the present can lead to future success. As a result, the goal provides a sense of direction, and the plan provides the momentum for getting there.

Jenny, a fifteen-year-old, has decided that she would probably like to be a writer and a teacher. She has taken many writing classes and is planning to assist a preschool teacher this summer. She will learn from her experiences, and they will facilitate the accomplishment of her goals.

The challenge is to set goals and then follow plans when they work out and perhaps modify them when they don't seem to be working. Good planning also involves some flexibility. Sometimes plans don't work out perfectly, so the ability to adapt and come up with alternatives is very important.

How can parents help this process? It is important that parents not impose their own goals on their children. If a child is not committed to a particular goal, he or she will probably not follow through on it. Parents can share their own life goals and the plans they made to help them attain those goals. They can offer support and encouragement when children set reasonable goals and make progress. When some plans don't work out, parents can help children deal with disappointments in a constructive manner. They can remind children of the goals they have set and of the work and energy required to reach those goals. They also can help children set worthy goals and point out some goals and motivations that are destructive and detrimental to society.

Parents cannot make children create goals. It doesn't help to pressure a child to come up with a list. However, taking time on a regular basis to discuss the importance of setting clear goals will give children the incentive they need to plan for the future.

A Word for Children

You can choose what you want to become and what you want to achieve.

Moving into Action

1. Parents, make a list of your personal goals—those related to physical health and well-being, spiritual

growth, relationships, career goals, intellectual goals, and emotional maturity. Help your children select one or two of these areas and make their own lists. Examples might be "I want to exercise for thirty minutes each day" or "I want to be able to run a mile at the end of next month." Each person in the family can name something they would like to accomplish in the next week, month, three months, or year.

2. Talk with your children about why you chose the goals you did. Which are short-term and which are long-term? What have you had to give up in order to attain your goals?

3. With your children discuss goals you set that did not turn out as you expected. Tell how you felt about that.

This one thing I do: forgetting what lies behind and straining toward what lies ahead, I press on toward the goal.
Philippians 3:13-14

2

DISCIPLINING YOURSELF, IMPROVING YOUR SKILLS

Thomas Edison, even after his 2000th attempt at inventing the lightbulb, knew the value of continued cooperation. His discouraged assistant complained, "All our work is in vain. We have learned nothing." Edison replied, "We have come a long way and learned a lot. We now know there are 2000 elements we cannot use to make a good lightbulb." When they finally succeeded in making a lightbulb that Edison thought would work, his nervous assistant dropped it. They worked around the clock and made another.
—Matthew and Dennis Linn, Sheila Fabricant

Becoming really good at something gives a person a sense of self-worth. Developing a talent and working hard to maintain a high level of accomplishment helps a person gain a sense of personal power. When people feel powerful and successful, they usually get noticed. Many violent people feel powerless and worthless. They engage in violent behavior as a way of feeling more powerful and perhaps receiving attention. Developing competence and mastery in children can prevent violence by providing success and power in healthy ways.

The greatest writers, inventors, athletes, musicians, and artists work hard and long hours. They practice their craft and work on improving their skills. There are drills that exercise the mind, body, and artistic spirit. Self-discipline is the key to success. Whether practicing a musical instrument or learning to placekick a football, practice often does make more perfect. In order to accomplish something worthwhile, you have to stick to it, try and try again, and learn from your mistakes. Thomas Edison invented the lightbulb only after many tries.

One of the challenges many young people face these days is the many distractions that tend to take them away from pursuing their goals. They find it easy to quit midstream and figure they have tried as much as they are going to try. Perseverance is the ability to keep focused, plug onward, and not let failures get in the way.

Self-discipline is sometimes considered an innate quality. Either a child has it or he or she does not. But others believe one can learn to be more disciplined and to keep on keeping on even without tangible signs of success.

Parents and teachers are important role models in encouraging children to be persevering. If the adults in a child's life demonstrate self-discipline and reap its rewards, the child will learn to do the same. Parents who spend hours practicing piano or guitar, exercising, or taking continuing education classes show their children that hard work does pay off. Continual practice may mean missing out on some fun. There are sacrifices to be made if one works hard at perfecting a skill. Children need to believe that the sacrifice is worth it. Parents can point out sacrifices they have made in the name of self-discipline and let their children know they are glad they did it.

It is important for parents to let children know the role that self-discipline has played in their lives. I have told my children several times that I took many writing classes and wrote hundreds of columns for free before I was asked to write books such as this one. My children have won a variety of musical and film contests because they have committed themselves to practicing and improving their skills.

Parents can support their children's development of self-discipline by helping them set up a practice schedule. However, the children need to participate in setting the schedule; it can't just be imposed by adults. Children especially need support and cheerleading when the going gets tough and immediate successes are not attained. "Keep at it," "Good job," and "I know you can do it" are all helpful responses. Adults can encourage children by pointing out how far they have come from when they started. While it is not in their best interests to have children become totally dependent upon adult praise, it is important to let them know that you are proud of their accomplishments and their hard practice. A support network of other children who are self-disciplined and are working toward achieving similar goals can also reinforce a child's willingness to practice. However, it is also important that children play and take breaks. If they are held to a too rigid schedule, they will feel deprived and possibly lose interest.

Children develop more self-discipline when they are motivated to do a task well. If it is their own idea, rather than their parents' idea, they take it more seriously and tend to work on it more diligently. As successes come, it is easier to maintain self-discipline. After a well-done piano recital, for example, a child might feel more motivated to keep practicing regularly.

A Word to Children

If you practice a lot and stick with it, you'll feel good about what you can do.

Moving into Action

1. Talk with your child about what it means to be self-disciplined. Share stories about your successes and how they related to self-discipline and perseverance.

2. Discuss specific goals both parent and child have about learning or improving a skill—such as playing a musical instrument or solving math problems. Create a practice schedule with your child.

3. With your child, focus on the good feeling that comes from improving one's skills. What are the benefits of working hard at something for a long time? How do you feel? When do you know you have done a task or project well?

4. Give younger children (under age eight) an opportunity to learn self-discipline by encouraging them to do simple tasks well, such as taking care of a pet, making their bed, or clearing the table of dishes. Talk about the good feelings people can feel inside when they do something worthwhile and notice a difference.

Every athlete in training submits to strict discipline in order to be crowned with a wreath that will not last; but we do it for one that will last forever.
1 Corinthians 9:25 TEV

3

BRAINSTORMING AND PROBLEM SOLVING

Life is difficult. Life is a series of problems to be solved.
—M. Scott Peck

C hildren learn early that life is not without its problems. There are always decisions to make, people to please, conflicts to resolve. Problems come when two people disagree, when obstacles get in the way, and when crises, losses, accidents, or illnesses occur. Some problems are simple. Others are complex.

The more skills a child has in coping with life's problems, the more likely he or she will achieve success and happiness. When violent people lack effective problem-solving skills, they become frustrated and enraged by problems. They then may act out in a violent manner.

As children experience problems, parents can help them by reassuring them that problems are part of everyone's life. Children can learn problem-solving skills and strategies from an early age. The variety of problems they may face includes academic and intellectual, interpersonal and emotional, and spiritual and physical problems. Here is a ten-step approach to problem solving that can be taught to any child above the age of five:

1. Recognize that there is a problem.
2. Name the problem.
3. Stand back and try to see the problem in a new way.

4. Lay out the issues that the problem presents. What are the choices? What are the conflicts or difficulties? What kind of solution would work?
5. Brainstorm a list of possible solutions
6. List the outcomes, both positive and negative, of handling the problem in particular ways.
7. Try one approach from your list that seems best.
8. Evaluate the results.
9. If one way to solve the problem fails, choose your next best option.
10. Be willing to accept that there may not be a "perfect" solution to the problem.

An example of a problem might be that your seven-year-old daughter, Jennifer, is planning a birthday party and really wants to invite her friend Alison but not Sandra, who is often disruptive during loosely supervised events. However, Alison and Sandra are best friends. It is possible that Alison won't come if Sandra isn't invited. It is also possible that Sandra will speak negatively about your daughter to Alison if she is not invited, and that may affect Alison's friendship with Jennifer. If Sandra is invited, she might ruin the party.

What are some possible solutions?

1. Jennifer could talk to Alison and tell her she really wants her to come. She might tell her that although she knows Alison and Sandra are friends, she is not inviting Sandra this time.
2. Jennifer could plan a more supervised party to which Sandra might come and at which she might not be as likely to be disruptive.
3. Jennifer could invite Alison to do something with just her. She could have a party without inviting Alison or Sandra.
4. Jennifer could forget the idea of having a party and just plan some event with Alison.

Each of these solutions might work. They require Jennifer to have good verbal and interpersonal skills and to be clear about her intentions. In each case, there is the possibility that the solution will be less than perfect. Jennifer has to consider what she is willing to settle for and which solution might cause the least problem or conflict.

All of these skills—verbalizing, brainstorming, imagining outcomes, analyzing, clarifying, and planning—can be taught to young children five years old or older. Parents can create role-playing situations for which they think up problems and help their children through the ten steps listed above. One example might be teaching children how to solve the problem of sharing a toy that each one wants to play with at the same time. Another example might be dealing with the problem of wanting to play outside but having to practice violin.

A Word to Children

We all have problems, but we can learn how to come up with ideas to solve them.

Moving into Action

1. Share with your child the kinds of problems people might experience during a lifetime. List some of the problems most likely to happen in childhood, adolescence, adulthood, and later adulthood. Help your child realize how much problems are a part of everyone's life.

2. Make a list of several problems in your life that are appropriate to share with a child. Then identify some problems in your child's life that need to be solved. Choose one problem from the parent list and one from the child list. Go through the ten-step process for each and try one or more solutions.

3. Preschoolers can be asked to solve simple problems: You have three cookies and want to share them with four of your friends. How do you do this? Or you and your friend Juanita both want to ride your tricycle at the same time. How do you solve this?

Get all the advice you can, and you will succeed.
Proverbs 15:22 TEV

4

COPING WITH DISAPPOINTMENTS BY GRIEVING, FORGIVING, AND BOUNCING BACK

The road to human development is paved with renunciation. Throughout our life we grow by giving up. We give up some of our deepest attachments to others. We give up certain cherished parts of ourselves. We must confront, in the dreams we dream, as well as in our intimate relationships, all that we never will have and never will be. Passionate investment leaves us vulnerable to loss.

—Judith Viorst

To be able to live a nonviolent life, one must learn effective means of coping with losses and disappointment. Life is not smooth for anyone. Children soon learn that life has its successes and failures, its joys and sorrows. Early in life, we separate emotionally from our parents. We aren't allowed to be babies anymore. We give up our special blankets and teddy bears. Friends move away. Our first pet dies. A grandparent dies. We get a bad grade on a test even though we studied diligently. One of our friends tells our secret to someone else. Someone teases us and calls us names. A group of friends has a party that excludes us. A neighbor gets cancer and becomes progressively weaker and more feeble. Our first love tells us that he or she loves someone else. As we age, we lose some relationships, and we lose parts of ourselves.

We lose romantic dreams, illusions of freedom and security, and the feeling of immortality. Loss is all around us.

In order to grow into nonviolent maturity, all of us need to learn the skills that help us cope with loss and disappointment in healthy ways. We can learn to accept that losses have occurred and will continue to occur. We can learn to grieve our losses, feel our feelings, and then move on, recover, and begin to live life fully again. It is healthy to feel the pain of loss, to grieve, and to be sad. Although we hope people will get over their losses, we realize that people are never the same once they have suffered a significant loss. We must learn to accept the reality of losses, forgive those who hurt, let go of anger and grudges, and move on.

Elizabeth Kubler-Ross, in *On Death and Dying,* writes about all the stages of the grief process, noting that we deny loss, get angry, bargain with God or some higher power, become sad or depressed, and ultimately accept the loss that has occurred. Children can be taught that grieving is a normal process that all human beings experience. We can be helped by guidance and support. When we go through a loss or disappointment, we can feel our feelings in a way that does not injure ourselves or others. We can learn to cope with the pain of loss by expressing our grief. As children and adults, we can learn to integrate loss into our lives—realizing that we have all experienced loss, but that we need to move on and get over it.

Coping with disappointment requires grieving, forgiving, and bouncing back. Those who are stuck in the anger phase of grieving have trouble forgiving. Violent children tend to be angry and hurting from some loss they have experienced. Getting over a loss does not mean minimizing or denying it. It means realizing that it is not good to dwell on the pain indefinitely. Sometimes parents may wish to seek professional help if they believe that their child's grieving has gone on for too long and seems unresolved.

Parents can help children cope with loss and disappointment by discussing the notion that loss is part of life. They can share some of the significant losses they have experienced and describe how they coped with them. Parents can give children the permission to grieve openly and also can encourage them to move on when it is time. When parents openly hold grudges against others, it does not encourage their children to forgive and move on.

Because people are unique in their grieving, it is difficult to say when one has grieved enough. It depends in part on the type of relationship one had with what has been lost. Closer friendships and relationships cause more pain when they are broken. Grieving also depends upon the way in which the loss occurred. We have expected losses, such as the loss of a ninety-year-old grandmother. We also have unexpected losses, like the loss of a fifteen-year-old sister in an automobile accident. Some grieving is anticipatory—when you know someone is going to die. In other cases, a sudden, shocking loss may cause more trauma. You may not have had any time to say goodbye.

But grieving takes place when a person experiences other disappointments, as well—a friend moving away, a bad grade, a teasing remark. We can lose our sense of hope, our dignity, our image of the how the world works. All of these losses can be causes for grieving. Hurt feelings are an everyday occurrence. Violent behavior is often a result of loss and pain, a person striking out at others or at him or herself after suffering some personal sense of loss.

In American society, boys are often discouraged from crying. This means that many boys and men bottle up their grief inside and never let anyone see their pain. As a result, some men resort to pain-numbing substances, such as alcohol, so they don't have to feel their pain. It is important that parents allow boys to cry, because crying will help move the process along. Boys should not be shamed for crying in public about their losses. But if parents are worried about others shaming their son, they can suggest to their son that he cry in private or only with those who will support him. If boys fear showing their pain and hurt, they may remain stuck in the anger phase of grieving and strike out at others or at themselves.

When disappointments come, it is easy for children to shame themselves into thinking they are incompetent, inadequate, or worthless. Parents can help their children realize that a disappointment does not mean inadequacy. Parents can teach their children to forgive others who hurt them, learn from their mistakes, and take disappointments in stride.

My friend Jeff's fourteen-year-old son was fired from his first job. He was very hurt and disappointed. Jeff and his son discussed how unfair his son felt the firing was and then talked about all the future jobs he would hold. His father asked him what he learned from his experience and how he might do things differently if he had another chance. His father shared with him the pain he felt when he was passed over for a promotion. It was an opportunity to meaningfully let the son in on a part of his father's life.

People can learn to support others during their grief. Here are some specific things to do or say:

1. Listening is vital.
2. Don't respond with glib statements such as "God must have wanted your brother in heaven." Say little. Don't judge. Let people know you are available to listen without judging or attempting to fix things.
3. Give physical affection, such as a hug, if the grieving person wants this.
4. Don't say, "I know exactly how you feel."
5. Ask what you can do to help.
6. Make yourself available. Be present even when they don't want to talk about the grief or loss. Let them know "If you want to talk, just call me."
7. Give hope and support: "I know you will work through this and everything will be okay."

Forgiveness can be modeled by parents in the home. Children can be encouraged to let go of their grudges and move on. Parents can discuss the process of forgiveness with their children, pointing out that holding grudges keeps a person stuck in the past and unable to move forward. Forgiving does not mean the person did not hurt you. It means that you no longer want to dwell on the pain that was caused, and you realize the person who hurt you is imperfect.

Forgiveness does not necessarily have to be done face-to-face. A child can learn to forgive someone in his or her heart. Children who experience bullying often have a difficult time empathizing with the bully and forgiving him or her. Most bullies suffer their own pain and disappointments. They are bullying out of a need to control so they don't feel that pain. While children won't always understand this, they need to let go of their desire to "get back at someone" and move to a state of forgiveness. Moving on beyond the pain and suffering in life is called resilience.

A Word to Children

Sometimes we lose what we love and don't get what we want. That's hard, but after we feel bad for a while, we can pick up and move on.

Moving into Action

1. Make a list of some of the greatest losses that you and your children have experienced. How have your family members grieved their losses? What are different ways you helped each other in the grieving process?

2. Talk to children about the need for physical self-care—getting enough rest, eating well, and exercising—when they experience losses. Have you ever neglected your body and become ill during these times?

3. Find out about possible support groups in your area for people grieving different types of losses.

4. Tell your children about ways in which you have bounced back. Tell them about your faith in second chances. Tell them that we can go through losses and recover, finding new joys in our lives.

5. Write down the names of people who have hurt you and create a ritual of forgiveness in which you toss the paper into a fire or tear it up. As you let go of your grudges, tell your family that you are letting go.

Blessed are those who mourn, for they will be comforted.
Matthew 5:4

5

ASKING FOR NURTURING AND CARE WHEN YOU NEED IT

A good relationship can help us become more whole,
but not in the magical way we often imagine. Instead,
by calling forth deeper qualities of our nature that we
have lost touch with, love also brings us up against
confining identities that normally cut off our access to
these qualities.

—John Welwood

Although there are some highly creative loners who are inventors, writers, or scientists, most of us want the company of other people in our lives. Evidence shows that many people who are violent are loners who lack supportive friendships. They live their lives in isolation. Sometimes they pretend to be so strong, independent, and in control that they believe their own facade. They don't learn how to socially interact and get little feedback about their own behavior. We are social creatures, a community, a people who need others for support, nurturing, guidance, love, encouragement, and appreciation. When we ask for nurturing and care, we admit that we cannot do everything for ourselves.

You can teach your children the importance of asking for nurturing and care when they need or want it. Nurturing includes attention, hugs, support, listening, holding, and comforting. It is not shameful or a sign of weakness to need this kind of assistance in our lives. Children can learn whom to ask, how to ask, and when to ask for nurturing. Not just anyone is capable of being or willing to be a nurturer. Children can make good choices and ask those who are both capable of and willing to nurture.

Nurturing can be given by a close friend. It can be offered by a parent or provided by a trained professional, within professional boundaries. Nurturing is available from teachers and mentors, from coaches and Scout leaders. Nurturing certainly can come from family members. Nurturing can also come from inanimate objects, such as a blanket or a favorite toy. Sometimes children have a difficult time asking for nurturing. They may think they are "too old" for such care.

When do we need nurturing? Some people need support, love, attention, and care every day. Others need it especially when they are going through a difficult time. Some people want it when they are ill or in crisis. Others want it when things are going well. Each of us has different attitudes toward nurturing and different wants and needs. It is helpful for a child to get in touch with this part of himself or herself.

What if no one is present to nurture? Nurturing can be done by long distance telephone calls or through cards and letters. Mary and Armondo, a couple I know, leave little caring notes in lunchboxes and in shirt pockets.

How do we wish to be nurtured? Some people respond well to verbal nurturing. Supportive words mean a lot. Others like physical support and reassurance, a hug, an arm around the shoulder, a pat on the back. Still others prefer gestures such as a look of support or approval. We can nurture someone by bringing them food or something to drink.

Can one ever be too dependent upon the nurturing of others? Certainly being nurtured can become an addiction like any other behavior. Often we can get by with self-nurturing. There are times when people have to plow through a situation without much support. However, violent individuals tend to have too little nurturing rather than too much.

Carlos enjoyed those big hugs his mother would give him when he came home from school. He decided that when he became a father, he would give his children those same big hugs he appreciated so much. Interpersonal connectedness gives children a sense of belonging and love. Feeling nurtured and supported is crucial for healthy, nonviolent emotional development. Asking for nurturing in appropriate places with appropriate people is a sign of maturity.

A Word to Children

When you need help and comfort from someone, it's a good thing to ask for it.

Moving into Action

1. What kinds of nurturing, support, and care does every human being need? Each family member can present one or two kinds of nurturing.

2. Name times when it makes sense to ask for nurturing.

3. What are the situations and reasons that a person might be hesitant to ask for nurturing from someone else?

4. What type of care do you like the best? Ask one member of your family to nurture you in a specific way in the coming week. You might ask for a neck rub, for some positive words of encouragement, or for some help with a task.

Ask, and it will be given you; search, and you will find; knock, and the door will be opened for you.
Luke 11:9

SELF-DEFENSE SKILLS

6

PROTECTING YOUR RIGHTS AND PRIVACY

Setting boundaries is about learning to take care of ourselves, no matter what happens, where we go, or who we're with. Boundaries emerge from deep decisions about what we believe we deserve and don't deserve . . . from the belief that what we want and need, like and dislike, is important . . . from a deeper sense of our personal rights, especially the right we have to take care of ourselves and be ourselves. Boundaries emerge as we learn to value, trust and listen to ourselves.

—Melody Beattie

Our children see aggressive behavior all around them. Newspapers detail violence and aggression between nations, groups, and individuals. Movies, television, and professional athletics graphically show aggressive behavior—from boxing to football, from shootings to bombings.

Children can learn the difference between aggressiveness and assertiveness. Aggressiveness means boldly taking things from others, invading people's space, bullying, intimidating, and violating boundaries. Assertiveness, on the other hand, means protecting what's yours: your rights, your privacy, your body, your space, and the rights of your family and your friends. Assertive people ask for what they want and express their needs and wants clearly. Being assertive involves speaking up, letting others know who and what you are and what you stand for. Healthy people feel good enough about themselves to share their thoughts, questions, and ideas.

Parents can develop a clear sense of their own boundaries and limits and can model boundary-setting behavior. For example, when Cesar and Lucinda's children, Sam and Michelle, were young, they would run unannounced into Cesar and Lucinda's bedroom in the mornings, jump on the bed, and cuddle together. As Sam and Michelle grew older, Cesar and Lucinda explained to them that their bedroom was their private space and could only be entered by knocking and then receiving permission to enter. At the same time, Sam and Michelle learned that they had a right to privacy in their own rooms and that parents needed to knock before entering.

Melody Beattie says that "the goal of having and setting boundaries isn't to build thick walls around ourselves. The purpose is to gain enough security and a sense of self to get close to others without the threat of losing ourselves, smothering them, or being invaded." When parents teach children how to set appropriate boundaries, children gain security and a sense of self-identity. If they learn that others have the same rights as they do to set and maintain clear boundaries, they then can respect the boundaries set by others as they wish to have their boundaries respected.

Some children are taught to please others at all costs. They may understand this to mean that they have no right to set limits or say no. Children who do not have clear boundaries sometimes grow up to be overly concerned about the needs of others and to ignore their own needs. They tend to give themselves away, losing themselves in relationships by making sure that others get everything they need while they receive nothing for themselves. They become so totally selfless that they fail to recognize when others might be manipulating or controlling them. As a result they may become either depressed or angry and rageful.

When she was twelve, our friends' daughter, Elizabeth, developed friendships with very needy people. When her parents asked her what she was getting from these relationships, she said she didn't know. After a while, she realized that some of these people were using her to avoid dealing with their own problems, and they were not respecting her time and energy. Elizabeth learned that she had enabled them to stay stuck and received very little for the time and effort she put in. After realizing that her needs were not being met, she began to limit her time with them and protect her rights.

In the process of setting boundaries, children need to learn how to cope with boundary invaders, people who violate and disrespect others' boundaries. When someone sets a clear boundary that is violated by someone else, a confrontation often occurs. The boundary setter might say, "This is not okay. You have no right to do this to me. I feel as though you are taking up all of my time and wanting all of my attention. I want to do other things and be with other people."

In order to set healthy boundaries, the following skills are required.

1. knowing one's own feelings, needs, wants, goals, and limits
2. being able to verbally express them to others and set clear boundaries around one's space, rights, privacy, and body
3. being aware when someone else is violating one's boundaries
4. recognizing anger and discomfort as possible signs that boundaries are either too weak, unclear, or not being respected
5. speaking up about the violation and enforcing the boundary
6. leaving a violating person or situation if necessary
7. finding supportive people who encourage one to set clear boundaries

8. supporting others in their setting of clear boundaries
9. changing boundary limits that seem inappropriate

As children move into adolescence, they are exposed to a wider range of people and situations. Learning to set clear boundaries as children is especially helpful as they grow older, leave home, cope with strangers, and move into the larger world. Their boundaries will be tested by others—friends, lovers, teachers, and employers.

Boundary violators are everywhere. Telemarketers call during your dinner hour and ask for contributions. Salespeople come to your door and assume you have time to listen to their pitch. (They rarely ask if this is a good time and rarely tell you their real purpose initially.) Boundary violators don't ask your permission. They interrupt your sentences and finish them for you. They stand too close, touch inappropriately, don't listen, and ask questions that are too personal.

Children can learn that not all people who violate their rights are evil or manipulative. Some people just don't understand the concept of boundaries and may not have any boundaries themselves. Other people may believe they have a right to other people's time, energy, or space. Discernment (a skill we will discuss in chapter 13 when talking about choosing good friends) helps children learn to make these distinctions.

A Word to Children

You have a right to protect your body, property, and ideas. Respecting yourself will help you respect the rights of others.

Moving into Action

Children need to practice protecting their rights and setting and enforcing their own boundaries. Teaching children to recognize boundary violators is very important.

1. Write a personal bill of rights in which children list the aspects of themselves they wish to protect.

2. Act out role-playing situations in which parents and children take turns defending their boundaries when someone infringes on their rights:

   a. Aunt Margaret comes for a visit and insists on being huggy and kissy with ten-year-old Jimmy. Jimmy doesn't want to be kissed and hugged. What might Jimmy say to Aunt Margaret? Suppose she tries to make Jimmy feel guilty if he doesn't kiss her on the lips. What can Jimmy say to that? What can Jimmy do if Aunt Margaret refuses to stop?

   b. Older brother Dan has a habit of interrupting Jesse's sentences. What can Jesse say to Dan to protect his right to finish his own sentences?

   c. Keisha, age sixteen, comes into her bedroom and discovers that her nine-year-old sister, Mia, is looking through her private papers. What could Keisha say to Mia?

3. How do you show respect for others' boundaries? You can model how to keep your distance, wait for people to finish what they are saying, stay out of people's private space, respect their bodies, etc.

4. Encourage children to learn about themselves, their needs, feelings, goals, desires, hopes, and dreams. Chapter 11 focuses on children learning to identify their own feelings. Have them draw pictures of themselves or write down some of their personal characteristics. Ask them to describe the boundaries they would like to set to protect their privacy, body, and other rights. Developing a strong sense of self is the first step toward being assertive and setting clear boundaries.

5. With your children, identify situations reported in newspapers or on TV in which boundaries have been violated, including the most serious as well as those that seem less serious. Examples include physical abuse, rape, inappropriate touch, breaking and entering, name-calling, harassment, and shaming. Discuss some of the problems that come from boundary violations and the penalties for the more serious violations.

6. Help children differentiate between aggressive and assertive behavior. Make two columns, labeling one "assertive" and the other "aggressive." Have the children list several behaviors that fall under each one. For example, under "assertive" they could write "Asking for what I want." Under "Aggressive," they could write "Taking something that doesn't belong to me."

Deliver me, O Lord, from evildoers; protect me from those who are violent.

Psalm 140:1

7

AVOIDING POTENTIALLY VIOLENT PEOPLE

Violence is best understood as developing out of an interaction between a biological potential and certain kinds of environments. . . . Peer pressure is important. Concerns with dominance and proving manhood through fighting can lead boys in groups to commit acts of violence that they would not commit on their own.

—Myriam Miedzian

There are people and situations that children need to learn to avoid. How can your child learn which situations and people are potentially dangerous, threatening, or abusive?

My wife and I believe that our actions speak louder than our words. We have shared with our children our reasons for not getting involved with an abusive person or leaving a situation that we believed to be abusive. We have talked about the potential dangers of trusting someone who does not really care about us. We also have explained that if you get involved with an abusive person, it is more likely that you will be abused or become involved in something potentially harmful to yourself and others. Young people who drink are more likely to be involved in auto accidents. People who have short tempers are more likely to rant and rave and get into trouble.

Maintaining a sense of personal values is very important. If a child knows what is important and what is right and what is wrong behavior, he or she is more likely to stay centered when temptations occur. Children who believe they are worthwhile are less likely to be coerced by peers into drinking, drugs, early sexual activity, speeding, or committing any violent acts. Helping to build this strong sense of self is an important part of parenthood. A child who knows that he or she is loved, accepted, and valued is more likely to have strong ethical principles and morals. The teaching and modeling of nonviolent parents helps children avoid potentially violent people and situations.

You can help your children avoid violent people and situations by teaching them to anticipate when something destructive might happen. Children can use their imaginations and think of the warning signs that a violent situation may occur. One example is when a child who appears quiet becomes belligerent, angry, and hostile. This might be a clear warning sign that a violent situation could erupt. Some children lack the ability to control their impulses. They do the first thing that comes into their minds, not thinking about consequences. By learning to identify children who act this way, your child can steer clear of troubling situations and volatile people.

Children who have low self-esteem and feel powerless about their own life situations sometimes try to exert power over others in negative ways. They learn to manipulate people. They get others into trouble by goading them and luring them to engage in destructive behaviors. Sometimes the goaders get off without punishment because they move to the sidelines. This type of manipulation can be observed, and children can learn how to recognize it.

Other children seem to seek excitement and have no real focus or purpose to their lives. They try to drum up arguments, fights, and trouble because they are used to having drama in their personal lives. They usually have poor boundaries and use aggressive behavior to take what they want. Children can learn to identify excitement junkies and avoid them.

Some adults in children's lives also can be violent, destructive, and abusive. Adults in positions of power and authority can use their status to take advantage of children's innocence—emotionally, physically, or sexually. Children can be taught to be strong enough to ask for help if and when they are approached by an unhealthy adult. Children sometimes don't ask for help because they don't think they will be believed. It is important to convey to your children that you will believe them and take their concerns seriously.

If your child is focused, mature, and responsible, it is possible that he or she will not be one of the most popular children. Children need to learn the difference between popularity and true, deep, committed friendship. A mature child often doesn't fit in with everyone. A child needs to be willing to give up popularity and pseudo-friendships when taking the "higher" route to maturity, compassion, and nonviolence. Parents can help children find other children with good self-esteem.

Sometimes children follow unhealthy leaders and learn later rather than sooner that those people are abusive and destructive. Although it is better to get out early, it is never too late to get out of a bad situation. Some children stay in bad situations because they are afraid to admit that they have participated in some destructive behaviors. Allowing your children to confess mistakes, accepting your children, and supporting their changes sends the message that one can always learn from past experiences and move to more mature, nonviolent behavior.

A Word to Children

You can learn to recognize dangerous people and places and stay away from them.

Moving into Action

1. What are some of the traits of children and adults who use their leadership to gain an unfair advantage over others? What are some warning signs that these people should not be trusted?

2. Demonstrate a situation in which a child or adult asks for trust but behaves in a way that shows he or she should not be trusted. An example of this might be a child claiming he or she needs another child's help to do something illegal.

3. A group of children decide to break into an empty house at night. These are children in your grade, and they pretend to be your friends. What can you say to these children as they try to tempt you into going along with them? What if the leader tries to put more pressure on you?

4. For younger children: Who is one dangerous person you can think of? What is one dangerous place you can think of?

Do not envy the violent, and do not choose any of their ways.

Proverbs 3:31

8

DISARMING THE BULLY

Mom, if you think your life is hard, you ought to be on the playground at recess.

—Joey, age 10

We all have experienced bullies in our lives. The bully might be your boss or the kid on the playground. It might be Uncle Peter who teases you and tells you what to do all the time when he comes to visit. It might be a gang of teens that roams your neighborhood.

In order to disarm the bully, we first have to understand why people bully others. Bullying is about intimidation and control. One reason bullies threaten or hurt others is because it gives them a sense of power. They must have power over others because deep inside they feel powerless, fearful, and inadequate. Many bullies lack other skills. Most bullies are very out of touch with their real feelings and don't want to face their powerlessness or pain. As a defense, they cover their pain with bravado and pretend to be strong and in control. By dominating someone else, bullies feel one-up. Underneath, they are hurting or fearful, with little sense of worth.

Sometimes people bully in groups or gangs because it gives them a feeling of connection or we-ness. Bullying is something they do together. It builds them all up, and they can gloat about who they have hurt or intimidated.

Bullying also is something to do for people who are bored and have no purpose or sense of direction. Bullying helps them avoid thinking about the lack of meaning in their lives.

Bullying provides a way of venting one's anger and frustration. It takes out one's rage on others. The release feels good temporarily.

Another reason people bully others is that bullies get their own way when they intimidate or control others. Others are frequently scared or look the other way. Since bullies can get away with their behavior, they think it proves that they are better or smarter than authorities.

What can be done to disarm the bully?

When I was bullied as child, I went to teachers and other authorities and told them what was happening. Most of them did little about it. A recent study by Bertus Ferreira, a criminal justice professor at Washburn University of Topeka, found that because of bullying nearly a third of high school students at three Midwestern schools wanted to transfer and 15 percent had considered suicide. Some victims of bullying turn violent themselves.

But schools are taking steps to reduce or eliminate bullying. Much more research is being done on the effects of bullying. Denver-area psychologists and social workers have developed a bully-proofing system, which is being used at Highline Elementary School. Potential victims are empowered with coping strategies, and the entire school community is behind the effort.

Denver-area social worker Paul Von Essen, from Cherry Creek, has created the concept of the "caring majority" of kids who are neither bullying nor being bullied. These children take the victim of the bullying gently by the arm and begin to include him or her in a group activity. They inform the teacher if someone is in trouble but don't tattle. Bullies then feel out of place and powerless. Their bullying doesn't work anymore.

How can kids "bullyproof" themselves? The creators of the Cherry Creek bullyproof program suggest that children who are challenged by bullies use the following strategies:

1. Offer help or give help to others.
2. Be assertive. Say, for example, "Stop making fun of me. It's mean and unfair. Stop it."
3. Use humor, such as "Yes, this is an ugly shirt."
4. Avoid bullies by walking away.
5. Find a supportive adult and tell them what is going on.
6. Tell yourself something positive that counteracts the bully's negative message.
7. Agree with what the bully says. For instance, someone might say, "You're right. I am a Native American. Do you want to know what our culture is really like?"

The Cherry Creek group also suggests that those who see someone being bullied could use the CARE strategy.

C: Creative problem solving. "You've been giving Johnny a hard time. Tell me something you actually like about him."

A: Adult help. Find an adult if someone might get hurt. Telling to protect someone is different from tattling to hurt someone.

R: Relate and join. "My clothes never seem to match, either. Some of us just don't have any fashion sense. It's kind of funny. But no matter what, we don't make fun of other people at this school."

E: Empathy. "You shouldn't say that about Jane. I'd be hurt if you said that about me."

You can order the complete guide to bullyproofing by calling (800) 547-6747.

Adults in authority can let children know they are not afraid to confront bullying when they see it or hear about it. It is important for children who are being bullied to know that the caring, supportive adults in their lives will help them.

A Word to Children

There are adults who can help you deal with bullies. You can avoid being bullied by being assertive, using humor, walking away, or telling yourself something positive that goes against what the bully says.

Moving into Action

1. Role-play a situation in which a bully has called you a name. Practice the strategy of avoiding the bully by ignoring what he or she says or leaving the situation.

2. Brainstorm assertive things you can say to a bully who calls you a name or teases you.

3. Help create a bullyproofing program in your school. Help the "caring majority" learn the techniques to end bullying.

4. Parents, share with your children incidents of bullying in your own lives and talk about the helpful strategies you used for coping with it.

Do not be overcome by evil, but overcome evil with good.
Romans 12:21

9

USING MEDIA WISELY

Television is a business. Broadcast TV is paid for by advertisers who have products and services to sell. . . . If I am going to grab and keep your attention, I have to do something to arouse you emotionally. . . . Certain things arouse emotions more reliably than others . . . violence, sex, and humor. Violence stimulates the adrenal glands . . . sexually oriented material stimulates us . . . humor [causes] changes in brain chemistry. . . . Every moment of television entertainment has to be arousing. As a result, programming is increasingly fast-paced. As children watch more and more TV, the machine gun pace becomes essential to keep them involved.

—David Walsh

Television is an incredible invention, a gift, a blessing from God. There are cable and educational channels to educate us about history, religion, science, and nature. In families, television can be used carefully and productively as a learning aid, offering opportunities for family interaction and discussion. Parents can view programs with children and discuss their implications. Television can be used to help children in making reports for school.

Television, like every other invention, also can be harmful if used inappropriately. David Walsh believes television uses sex and violence to stimulate its adult and child audience. In February 1996, results from a 1.5 million-dollar study funded by the cable TV industry were published in news-papers around the country. Based on a scientifically selected sample of 2500 hours of programming, it found

- Fifty-seven percent of the programs contained some violence.
- Perpetrators of violent acts on TV went unpunished 73 percent of the time.
- Most violent portrayals failed to show the conse-quences of a violent act.
- Twenty-five percent of the violent incidents on TV involved the use of handguns.
- Only 4 percent of the programs emphasized nonviolent alternatives in solving problems.
- The most violent Saturday children's programs con-tained from 70 to 130 violent acts per hour.

As children watch this much violence, they may become desensitized to it. They rarely see violent perpetrators empathiz-ing with their victims. Television also has a tendency to simplify complex problems, because a thirty-minute program needs to come up with a solution in thirty minutes. From watching television, children can learn unhealthy habits and develop a false idea of how the world works. In some cases, they may be taught that

- wealth will make you happy
- women are primarily sex objects
- it is manly to carry and use weapons
- walking away from a confrontation is a sign of cowardice
- products instead of character determine one's identity
- crude language, substance abuse, and infidelity are normal
- adults, especially parents, are stupid or boring
- athletes and movie stars are the people to be most admired

- casual sex is normal
- swearing by children is acceptable
- life is just about having fun

Although we can get depressed about these messages, we must keep in mind that parents are the primary educators of their children. Strong parental support and guidance can overcome any unhealthy messages that children see in the media. One way to ensure this is to be proactive in your belief that life is more interesting and complicated than most media present it to be. Doing, living, sharing, giving, communicating, and loving are active ways to combat the negativity and violence that may appear on the television or movie screen.

Things to keep in mind:

1. Using media wisely means monitoring what children watch. If you are uncertain about the amount of coarse language, sexuality, or violence in a particular television program, watch it once with your child.

2. If you decide that the program is promoting negative messages about what it means to live a healthy life, explain to your child just what you find objectionable about it. Give your child an alternative— something else to watch or something else to do.

3. If your child is going to friend's house, find out from the parents which videos they might be renting and watching. Since many children don't want to appear different from others, do your best to find family friends who have the same values as you do to reinforce your strategy. The argument from children that "nobody else cares what their children watch" is untrue, but you must work to prove that to your child.

4. Limit the amount of TV viewing. Too much TV watching and video game playing can promote passivity and the belief that a child must be plugged into

something in order to be entertained. Many parents I have met through workshops believe that one hour a night is plenty of television time.

5. Provide alternative activities—sports, discussions, group games, hobbies, creative classes, music lessons—that give children a chance to interact with others.

6. Provide healthy role models—productive, mature adults who are not preoccupied with sex, who do not seek violent confrontations, and who are aware of life's complexities. Find people who make genuine contributions to their communities, who are spiritually involved, and who are caring and loving to their friends and family. Healthy, mature men and women are not consumed by their appearance or by what type of car they drive. Some communities have created "Ordinary Hero Award" programs, in which they give awards to community volunteers and adults who have made a genuine difference in other people's lives.

7. Write to advertisers who sponsor violent programs, and boycott their products. Let them know that you will work to share your point of view with other parents who want to raise healthy and peace-loving children.

8. Don't give in to fads and promotions in which movies sell toys to promote themselves. There is often peer pressure to own the latest this or that. What has worked well with my children is to remind them that the previous "in" things didn't stay "in" for very long. Some kids have closets full of "in" things gathering dust.

9. Teach nonviolent conflict-resolution skills that are more effective than fists, knives, or guns. Much of this book is about providing skills that allow children

to use their minds rather than a weapon to navigate through the world.

10. Practice what you preach. This means being as vigilant about your own choices of viewing as you are about your children's choices. It is helpful to set a good example and avoid overly violent programs yourself.

A Word to Children

You can have fun and learn a lot from television but only if you use it wisely.

Moving into Action

1. Go through the television listings in your newspaper and find the programs that have valuable and healthy content. Decide together as a family which of those programs you might like to watch.

2. Watch two programs together that are shown during the "family hour." Make a list of the acts of violence, incidents of coarse humor, or examples of unhealthy behavior you observe during these programs.

3. Write a letter to an advertiser who uses sex or violence to promote a product. Let them know what you don't like about the ad and that you plan to boycott their product.

4. Make a list of your family guidelines for healthy television and movie viewing. You might include "programs that show an understanding of people's differences," "programs that treat people with respect," "programs that do not stereotype people into narrow roles," and "programs that show nonviolent ways of dealing with conflict."

Fill your minds with those things that are good and that deserve praise: things that are true, noble, right, pure, lovely, and honorable.

Philippians 4:8 TEV

10

CREATING SAFER SCHOOLS AND NEIGHBORHOODS

Neighborhoods with high crime rates and high rates of violent behavior pose a higher risk that children who live there will engage in violent behavior themselves. In these environments, children see violent behavior modeled on a frequent basis. . . . A child who comes from a very healthy family and who lives in a community where violence is not condoned has less risk for violent behavior.

—David Walsh

Violence occurs everywhere, and our schools are no exception. We know that all parents want their children's schools to be safe places, but violence occurs in our schools at alarming rates. There are fights on the playgrounds, shaming and ridiculing in the cafeteria, and bullying in the restrooms. There is name calling that goes on verbally and through note passing. Some children express their anger and frustration by abusing other children.

During the entire year of fourth grade, my chair was kicked by the person sitting behind me. It was done regularly, daily, and repeatedly. I told the teacher that this was happening, and nothing was done. The teacher thought it was a trivial matter. Yet it made it difficult for me to concentrate, and I know my grades suffered as a result of it. It also made me not want to go to school. The boy kicking my chair knew it bothered me and continued to do it for that very reason. While some people might not consider this violent behavior, it did affect my attitude toward school, authority, and learning and my feeling of safety. The kicker seemed delighted to get away with it, and it gave him a sense of power over me.

A government study reported that in United States schools in 1996 there were 10,000 physical attacks or fights with weapons, 7000 robberies, and 4000 sexual assaults. President Clinton commented, "The threat of such violence hangs over children's heads and closes their minds to learning." As a result, the U.S. Justice Department earmarked 15.5 million dollars for a new community policing program to address school safety.

Many schools are attempting to curb violence through antiviolence programs. Numbers of schools teach mediation skills through designed curricula that include role-playing. Other schools have stiff penalties for students who harass or abuse other students. Still other schools have programs in what is called "character development." This violence prevention program teaches children feelings identification, empathy skills, and respect for others, as well as additional skills. In some school settings violence prevention is approached through self-esteem building. The skills in this book are taught to some children throughout the country.

In some school programs, children are taught to recognize the harmful effects of violence in the media. They view and discuss videos for their violent and destructive content and learn to make healthy and appropriate choices. Many parent-teacher organizations sponsor "Turn Off the Television" Day or offer workshops for parents about raising nonviolent children. Some teachers may encourage collaborative learning, in which the focus is on learning with and from each other, rather than competing.

Some questions you might want to ask your children's teacher and principal include

1. What is the school's policy toward harassment and violence?
2. What programs exist to teach and encourage nonviolent behavior?
3. How do teachers encourage students to work cooperatively in groups?
4. If the school is involved in "character development" education, what are the personal traits that are being encouraged and how are they being modeled and taught?
5. What procedures are parents to follow if their child reports that he or she has been hurt, shamed, or harassed?
6. What are the punishments for violent behavior?
7. How carefully are children monitored on the playground, in the restrooms, and in the cafeteria?

Parents can become involved in community organizations such as those sponsored by the Search Institute of Minnesota, an organization that studies assets children need to be productive citizens. One example is a program called "Our Community, Our Youth" in Minnetonka, Minnesota. It encourages community leaders, parents, and educators to get together to discuss how to value and reward the healthy, nonviolent behavior of its youth. A variety of programs result, including "We Love Our Youth" Month with special programs about youth.

Many of these types of programs foster school and community partnership in creating safe spaces for children to learn. School parent-teacher organizations often have programs that foster student learning of respect and healthy communication skills. Parents can engage in discussions with school personnel about harassment and help create guidelines for school policies.

In addition to school violence, some children live in violent neighborhoods. There are drug deals that go bad, domestic disputes that end in violence, bank robberies, and assaults. What can parents do when their neighborhood contains violence?

Some move. Others work with their community to develop antiviolence programs. They institute Crime Watch programs and establish "safe houses" that children can run to in case of emergency. There are athletic and enrichment programs held after school that keep children engaged in worthwhile activities under supportive adult leadership.

Other communities develop Big Brother and Big Sister programs in which adults provide mentoring for children and adolescents. Although these are not antiviolence programs, they are dedicated to fostering positive self-esteem, altruistic and considerate values, and productive activity. The Search Institute's programs celebrate the strengths of young people and encourage adults to take responsibility for the youth in their community. Activities, special events, and guest speakers that encourage healthy behavior in children and adolescents are provided.

Some questions you might ask about your community include

1. What programs are available to youth?
2. What can our community do to encourage mentoring and taking responsibility for the safety and well-being of its children?
3. What types of role models that demonstrate peacemaking, generosity, and concern for others does our community place in front of youth?

We have a long way to go before all of our schools and neighborhoods are safe places for all children. Grassroots groups are working diligently at making these things happen. They need everyone's help—from political leaders to business leaders, from parents to teachers and spiritual leaders. The first step is to take violence seriously. The second is to create prevention programs that work, and the third is to find resources, both monetary and human, to implement these programs. By learning the skills in this book, children can help to make their schools and neighborhoods more peaceful places.

A Word to Children

We want our neighborhoods and schools to be safe places for everyone. You can help see where the dangerous places are and learn how to be safe.

Moving into Action

1. Do an assessment of your own community. Walk around the neighborhood as a family. Ask yourselves the following questions:

   How safe is our neighborhood?
   What are the danger spots?
   When and where do we feel threatened?
   What can we as a family do to make our neighborhood more safe?
   Is there a block program?
   Is there a neighborhood watch?
   Do we feel protected by the police?

2. Contact your local legislators and express your concerns about your neighborhood's safety.

3. Mobilize your neighbors to discuss safety issues. Have a town meeting.

4. Do an assessment of your schools. Find out if there have been any charges of harassment. How were they dealt with? Learn about school policies and practices.

5. Talk to the principal or a guidance counselor about starting a program of respect and character education.

6. Have a violence prevention month in your community or school. Sponsor activities, programs, and speakers about nonviolence.

7. Learn more about the programs and publications of Search Institute, 700 S. Third Street, Minneapolis, MN 55415-1138; phone (612) 376-8955 or (800)-888-7828; www.search-institute.org

Blessed are the peacemakers, for they will be called children of God.

Matthew 5:9

INTERPERSONAL SKILLS

11

IDENTIFYING FEELINGS AND EMPATHIZING WITH OTHERS

If we are truly to trust life we are going to need to learn to rely on friends and ask them for comfort. We are going to need to learn to share our feelings of loneliness, fear and hope with others.

—Anita L. Spencer

Many violent people are able to express only anger. They often are not in touch with other feelings such as sadness, loneliness, or fear. As a result, they bottle up all the other feelings, and the anger spills out as rage or violence.

Raising nonviolent children requires that each member of the family learn to express and share his or her feelings. There may be times when personal feelings are best kept private. However, being able to discuss what you are feeling within a family is a first step to providing the support that everyone needs.

Being able to identify and share feelings helps family members understand each other and give each other the necessary support to cope with the variety of life circumstances—the joys, the struggles, the disappointments, the transitions, the losses, and the successes. For healthy spiritual growth and development, it is important that each member of a family learn to identify his or her feelings and then be able to clearly express them to others in the family at appropriate times and places. Although this may be changing, girls are usually socialized to be able to express all feelings except anger. Boys, on the other hand, are encouraged to express anger but not share feelings of fear, sadness, loneliness, or joy. To be a truly healthy, nonviolent, and fully functioning family, both genders need to learn how to express all feelings.

It is important that parents act as role models for expressing a wide range of feelings. Some feelings may be inappropriate to share in front of the children and may be more appropriately shared with one's spouse. However, children benefit from seeing adult males and females expressing all types of feelings and being comfortable enough to share them in the proper environment.

When Grandpa Ralph died, the St. John family members each grieved in a different way. Ralph's son, James, was not able to openly cry in front of his family. He did, however, tell them that his father's death made him sad. Betty, Ralph's daughter, openly wept when she heard the news of his death. She also cried at the funeral service. Timothy, James's son, saw Betty crying and realized that he too could share that depth of feeling during the funeral.

How to identify one's own feelings is a skill that can be learned very early. First, a person must know that he or she is feeling something. The clue to the feeling may be a physical reaction. Fear may manifest itself as a queasy feeling in your stomach. Anger may be felt more in your neck and shoulders. Your eyes often well up with tears. You can help your children by teaching them to look for these kinds of cues that they are feeling something.

They then need a "feeling word" vocabulary from which they learn to put words to the sensations they are experiencing. Roland and Doris Larson have listed hundreds of feeling words in *I Need to Have You Know Me*. These range from *aggravated* to *afraid*, from *anxious* to *astounded*.

They include b*etrayed, calm, cheerful, confused, crushed, disappointed, encouraged, enraged, flustered, frantic, helpless, hopeful, hurt, intimidated, lost, nervous, overjoyed, petrified, pressured, relaxed, stunned, surprised, trapped, violated, vulnerable, weary,* and *zonked out.*

My wife and I have always tried to discuss feelings with our children, even when they were very young. After an interaction with someone, we would discuss how the person felt and what might have made them feel that way. Our children gained a sensitivity to the feelings of others as we discussed motivations and the impact of people's behavior on others. We also tried to teach them that in some circumstances it is safer to hold back your feelings. My son learned that sharing feelings on the soccer field was not always accepted by his friends. When he missed a ball, we could tell he was disappointed but he tried to focus on getting back in the game. Later, in private, he shared with us how he felt.

Children need to learn how to express their feelings appropriately in certain settings. Acting out rage may be therapeutic in private. However, in a public place, it can prove embarrassing. Parents can teach when it is helpful to express something in public and when it is important to keep one's feelings to oneself. This can be done by carefully considering which expressions of feeling might result in criticism or ridicule or which might hurt others and therefore are better kept to oneself until it is safe to let them out. Yelling, crying, pouting, and gesturing are all ways that facilitate getting our feelings out. Clearly some of these will be disruptive under certain circumstances. Learning when to express feelings and when to keep them inside is part of growing into a mature, healthy human being.

Being able to clearly express your feelings can lead to empathy, an important skill because it builds bridges between people. Having empathy involves understanding someone else's situation and caring about him or her. If you empathize with others, you will have some sense of what they are feeling. You care about them and want to help them feel better. You might first show caring by being with them as they feel whatever it is they are feeling. Then you might try to support and encourage them through verbal or physical reassurance.

In order to empathize with another person, it is helpful to put your own feelings on hold temporarily, so you can effectively "tune in" to his or her feelings. You show that you are empathizing by how you respond to the feelings of others. A perceptive person is able to listen and communicate both understanding and support. He or she can empathize with people from a wide range of backgrounds, ages, and situations. Understanding the feelings of others helps people become sensitive to others' needs, wants, and situations. If you see that Sarah is crying because Johnny made a mildly negative comment to her, you might become aware of Sarah's sensitivities and vulnerabilities and stop making such comments to her yourself.

Empathetic understanding is necessary for nonviolence. Family members and friends who ignore each other's needs and feelings cause resentment, and resentment leads to anger, rage, and possibly violent behavior. When family members and friends support each other emotionally, trust and mutual understanding is encouraged.

A Word to Children

It is important to understand a wide range of your own feelings so you can better understand and care about what others are feeling.

Moving into Action

1. Write a dozen feeling words—*happy, sad, lonely, scared, disappointed, excited, frustrated, surprised,*

angry, etc.—on slips of paper and put them into a hat. Select one feeling word and act out the feeling. Take turns guessing which feeling is being presented.

2. Create a role-playing situation in which two family members have a disagreement about where to go on vacation or which television program to watch. After each has spoken, discuss the feelings each shared and the kind of response that would have demonstrated empathy.

3. Practice listening to each other express a variety of feelings. As a feeling is expressed, notice the tone of voice, gestures, and facial expressions that accompany each feeling.

4. Read a short passage from a novel, such as *Tom Sawyer,* that expresses a variety of feelings. Try to express in words what the characters are feeling.

5. Sometimes when we are angry, we are also hurt or scared. Consider a time when you felt angry. Try to list some of the other feelings that you might have been feeling at the same time.

6. When you are reading a story aloud to your child, stop and ask, "How do you think this character is feeling? What could you say to him?"

Rejoice with those who rejoice, weep with those who weep.

Romans 12:15

12

RESPECTING OTHER PEOPLE'S RIGHTS

If children live with criticism,
*   they learn to condemn.*
If children live with hostility,
*   they learn to fight.*
If children live with ridicule,
*   they learn to be shy.*
If children live with shame,
*   they learn to be guilty.*
If children live with tolerance,
*   they learn to be patient.*
If children live with encouragement
*   they have confidence.*
If children live with praise,
*   they learn to appreciate.*
If children live with fairness,
*   they learn justice.*
If children live with security,
*   they learn to have faith.*
If children live with approval,
*   they learn to like themselves.*
If children live with acceptance and friendship,
*   they find love in others.*

—Dorothy Law Nolte

We expect very young children to be self-centered. See-ing beyond themselves into the needs, feelings, and rights of others requires an ongoing developing maturity. You can help your children to mature in this way by teaching them to respect the rights of others and by modeling this respect yourself.

One of the greatest problems the United States faces is the self-centeredness of many of its youth and adults. Some adults act like two-year-olds when driving their automobiles on the highways. They speed, tailgate, and cut off others. Some adults refuse to grant others the freedoms and rights they themselves take for granted. These people are so absorbed in their own world and problems that they choose not to see beyond their own selfish interests and desires. Their primary question about everything is, "How does it affect me?"

Lack of respect for someone's rights can result in violating their boundaries (see chapter 6). Some people become victimized, getting stepped on, ridiculed, and violated by others. They may be discounted and trivialized, be constantly interrupted, be forced to touch others against their will, or be touched by them. Some people become ruthless, cut into line, and push others out of the way. Taking things from others is an example of a boundary violation.

If we wish to raise nonviolent children in this violent world, we need to teach them about the needs, rights, boundaries, and feelings of others. When you show respect for your children by the way you talk to them or honor their space or their feelings, you are doing what is most important and effective in teaching them to respect others. Even three-year-old children are capable of developing respect and empathy, an understanding of the rights of others and compassion for them. They can be taught that other people they know—and even complete strangers—have the same rights as they have. Children can learn to understand the plight of those less fortunate and those who are ostracized, shunned, and ignored. Parents can explain how some children don't have the resources, freedoms, and possibilities that others have. Children can realize that their friends and acquaintances wish to have the same rights as they wish to have.

One way to teach this is to model it in the family. As our children were growing up, my wife and I consistently verbalized how we respected each other's rights, including privacy and space. We would point out to our children how we each had our own projects and each needed quiet time and privacy to work on them. If we wanted to read what the other wrote, we would always ask permission. Our children learned how to respect other people's boundaries because theirs were respected by the adults in the house.

How can your child learn to respect the boundaries, rights, privacy, and feelings of others? First, your child must understand that there are a variety of points of view and that people have a right to express their views even if they are not popular or politically correct. Not everyone feels the way they do about certain aspects of life.

Then, your child can develop an attitude of fairness, believing that others deserve the same rights your child wants for him or herself. This attitude can be taught by having parents explain how they take the needs and feelings of others into account. Parents can talk about why they don't call their friends during the dinner hour or don't invade the privacy of family members. Parents can set a good example by not barging into their children's rooms unannounced, without knocking first and asking permission to enter.

An attitude of caring for others is an important component of respecting rights and boundaries. An attitude of respect for others comes from watching adults who demonstrate this respect through their behavior.

Respecting others' rights and boundaries involves the following behavior.

1. listening without interrupting
2. not pushing, hitting, or shoving another
3. not offering unwelcome physical or sexual advances
4. not taking what doesn't belong to you

5. respecting the privacy of someone else's mail by not opening or reading it
6. not speaking for anyone else
7. not ridiculing, shaming, or condemning another's thoughts, feelings, ideas, dress, or appearance
8. knocking before entering a private space
9. asking permission before using something belonging to someone else
10. respecting a no the first time it is spoken

A Word for Children

If you think about how you like to be treated and treat others that way, you will probably be respecting their rights.

Moving into Action

Plan to spend a half hour discussing how one cares and demonstrates concern for others and why we need to respect others' rights just as we wish them to respect ours.

1. How do we show others we respect their rights? What are five ways that you show respect for the rights of other people in your family?

2. You see Niko and Jenny playing with a ball on the playground. Niko grabs the ball from Jenny and runs away with it. What do you do about it?

3. Poor people have less space, less privacy, and generally receive less respect than wealthy people. What is your responsibility to help protect the rights of poor people?

4. Parents, share with your child how you respect their rights by respecting their privacy. Give some examples.

5. Create a two-person role-playing situation in which you interrupt your child constantly, telling your child

what he or she is feeling. Let your child respond with how it feels when this happens.

Owe no one anything, except to love one another; for the one who loves another has fulfilled the law.

Romans 13:8

13

CHOOSING GOOD FRIENDS

Our job is not to control our children's social envi-
ronment. Rather, our work is to equip our children to
do that for themselves. When young people feel fool-
ish and worthless, when they don't like themselves,
when they are frightened by the threat of ridicule or
rejection, they are highly vulnerable. They are at great
risk of being led into any way of thinking, feeling, and
acting by the influence of peers.
　　　　　　　—John Crudele and Dr. Richard Erickson

Some people act violently because they are hanging around with angry, rageful, and violent friends. Other violent people have been reported to be isolated and friendless. They don't seem to have learned to emotionally connect with people and find caring, supportive friends. It is unclear whether isolation leads to violence or whether violent behavior leads to isolation. In any case, choosing good friends is a vital skill that all children need. Children who select friends wisely can have long-lasting relationships that bring them years of caring and understanding.

Children who choose good friends tend to have a sense of self-worth. They are comfortable with themselves, feel worthwhile, and appreciate their strengths. These children can acknowledge and accept their limits and shortcomings without letting them dominate their self-concepts. Parents can help their children learn how to wisely select those with whom they will be vulnerable. Close, trusted friendships evolve out of trial and error. Parents who have chosen good friends can share with their children how and why they made those choices.

What does one look for in a good friend? Valuable and trusted friends are consistent in their behavior. They maintain confidences and, above all, respect their friends and treat them well. Healthy friendships involve honesty, loyalty, and fairness. This means that one's good friends take a fair share of the responsibility for calling and for setting up activities. They tend to enjoy many of the same types of hobbies.

Children can learn to observe patterns of behavior in friends and then realize that although they can be kind to all children, they can choose to spend more time with those children who are going to treat them with respect and fairness. Sometimes children choose friends who are too busy and already have an overload of friendships. A very popular child may be spread too thin to be a good friend to your child.

My wife and I have tried to teach our children how to be a good friend to their friends once they have chosen them. We have individual friends and couple friends and try to maintain contact with them regularly. We demonstrate our caring for our friends by calling them and checking in, asking, "How are you doing?" Our children now do this type of caring on their own. If we have a good friend who is going through a difficult time, we spend extra time with them on the phone or in person. We both believe that children learn a lot from watching how their parents interact with their friends.

Parents can let their child know that they like a particular friend because he or she is loyal, honest, consistent, and trustworthy. However, it is important to stand back and let your child determine what makes a good friend, rather than deciding that for him or her. Sometimes too much parent involvement gets in the way of good friendships.

Here are twelve suggestions that parents can share with their children about choosing good friends wisely:

1. *Attract a friendship.*
   Let people know you are interested in becoming their friend. Invite them to do something.

2. *Avoid controlling and manipulative friends.*
   Learn to be wary of bossy and domineering children who always want to get their own way. Look for friends who are good thinkers and listeners as well as talkers. Choose children who are able to give and take. Let those children who would control you know that you are your own person, with your own feelings and ideas.

3. *Avoid needy and demanding children.*
   Whiny, dependent, and immature children often cling to friendships. They are difficult to leave because they use guilt and other ways of manipulating. Children need to be polite and tactful when they tell someone they do not choose to be close friends.

4. *Avoid angry, rageful friends.*
   Some children are angry because they feel unloved, unsupported, and neglected. These children often use friendships to feel better about themselves. However, their anger may come out in self-destructive acts or hurtful things that they do to their friends. Be aware of these behaviors.

5. *Try to change an unsatisfying friendship.*
   Tell the person that you are not happy with the friendship. Be specific about what you would like to see change. Give the person a specified amount of time to make his or her part of the changes. If, after that time, no changes are made, you can let them know that the friendship is not working for you.

6. *Move on from an unsatisfying friendship.*
   Be clear and specific about why you need to move

on. Let the person know that you still have some feelings for him or her, but right now being friends is not fulfilling your needs. You do not need to feel responsible for listening to all of the person's feelings. You can acknowledge that you understand it is difficult for him or her.

7. *Cope with rejection.*

Realize that not all people you want to befriend will necessarily feel that way toward you. Try not to take it personally, although this is difficult to do. Look for other people who are happy to see you and spend time with them.

8. *Make smart and careful friendship choices.*

Don't make your choice of friendships based on how a person looks or what kinds of material things they possess. Some particularly attractive people may not have the social skills necessary for good friendship.

9. *Learn to trust your instincts.*

When you have the feeling that the other person is not concerned about your interests, trust your innermost feelings. Look for warning signs that verify what you are feeling.

10. *Learn from your mistakes.*

When you misjudge somebody and they turn out to hurt or betray you, realize that you can learn something from everything. Look back over your history with that person and note the warning or danger signs that you ignored. Make a point of being more aware in the future.

11. *Be a good friend to your friends.*

Be the kind of friend you want them to be. Be interested in your friends. Take time to listen to them. Do some things they like to do. Be supportive and caring.

12. *Help your friends make good friends.*

Teach your friends some of what you have learned about making good friendships.

A Word to Children

We all need good friends who will care about us. Using thought and care in choosing good friends will make your life a lot happier.

Moving into Action

1. For both parents and children: Make a list of five qualities that you look for in a good friend. Make a list of five qualities you have that make you a good friend.

2. Parents, discuss with your children what qualities they would like to develop in themselves that would make them better friends to their friends.

3. For both parents and children: List three friends you have made in the last few years. What made you choose these people? Are they still good friends with you? What qualities make for a lasting friendship.

4. Parents, discuss these situations with your children.

   a. Latisha used to be your best friend. You played together nearly every day. Then, Angela moved next door. Now Latisha plays with Angela and says she doesn't want to be your friend anymore. What do you do?

   b. You really enjoy playing with Mike because he's good at soccer and has a great collection of video games. But Mike always has to win and puts you down every time you make a mistake. How do you handle that?

Make no friends with those given to anger, and do not associate with hotheads, or you may learn their ways and entangle yourself in a snare.

Proverbs 22: 24-25

14

EXPRESSING IDEAS AND LISTENING TO OTHERS

Words are very potent; they can be used to create a variety of outcomes. There are words that hurt, words that heal. . . . There is creative power in your every word. Use that power to draw the very best into your life and the lives of others.

—Douglas Bloch

One of the reasons people use their fists is because they don't know how to use their reasoning and their voices. Nonviolent behavior involves the abilities to express oneself and to listen effectively to others. This results in cooperative effort, collaboration, and win-win solutions to problems.

We communicate with words, gestures, eye contact, posture, and facial expressions. Sometimes our communication is complicated. We may say one thing, but our bodies may convey a different message. Children can be taught how to communicate their thoughts, ideas, and feelings in a clear and concise manner. To do so, they must understand what they are trying to communicate and learn a vocabulary that accurately conveys this. This comes from observing adults and other children. They also can learn how to get an idea across and how to make sure what they have said has been heard correctly.

I have taught my children how important it is to truly listen to another person. We have discussed the importance of active listening and have practiced listening, maintaining eye contact, and paraphrasing to let the other person know that he or she has been heard. My children have learned ways to let people know they are paying attention and truly listening to what is being said. Giving verbal and nonverbal feedback lets the person know you hear what they are saying and understand it.

Gladys Folkers, in her book *Taking Charge of My Mind and Body,* suggests that adolescents use "I" messages to express their wants and needs. "I" messages do not put the other person on the defensive and yet get across the message. As examples she gives "I have a problem with . . ." and "I'm concerned about . . ." Healthy communication is not a one-way street. It involves give-and-take and a willingness of two or more people to work toward understanding each other.

The first question to discuss is, Why communicate? The answer: because people need to understand each other in order to work together harmoniously. The next question is, When communicate? The most effective communication occurs when people have the attention, time, and energy to speak clearly and listen to each other. In some cases, it is helpful to set aside specific times to bring up complicated issues. Much miscommunication occurs when people are running out the door or have their mind on three other things. The third question is, How communicate? Here the answer is communicate face-to-face, with privacy.

There are different types of messages that need to be communicated. Here are just a few:

- communication about daily events and scheduling
- sharing personal needs and feelings
- communication about future goals and intentions
- coping with disagreements and conflicts
- social chitchat
- discussions of current affairs or politics

It is important that family members share the purpose for their communication and what they expect from the listener. Frequently people want validation and support but end up getting suggestions they aren't seeking.

The following are eight guidelines for effective family communication.

1. Set aside an adequate amount of time to discuss what you have to discuss.
2. Tell the listener why you are telling him or her what you are and what you expect back.
3. Be willing to listen and accept feedback.
4. Clarify your thoughts if the listener doesn't quite understand.
5. If the conversation is unfinished due to time constraints, set a future time to continue it.
6. Listeners should pay full attention and let the speaker know that they hear him or her.
7. Express appreciation for clear presentations and good listening.
8. Don't interrupt or finish each other's sentences.

Some families encourage communication at the dinner table when everyone is present. Others set up specific times for family meetings.

A Word for Children

If you can express yourself clearly and listen well to others, you will avoid many misunderstandings.

Moving into Action

1. Have two people set aside fifteen minutes of uninterrupted time in a quiet place. During that time they should discuss a topic—for instance, setting up plans

for the weekend—and practice the eight guidelines on page 93 during the discussion.

2. Create a role-playing situation in which parent and child disagree about whether what the child has just done is helpful or unhelpful. Use "I" messages instead of "you" messages when speaking.

3. Take turns being the speaker and the listener. Practice talking about something that is important to you. Give the listener time to think about a response. Have the listener paraphrase what the speaker has said. Then the speaker should let the listener know whether the speaker was heard correctly. If not, the speaker should repeat with more clarity what was said.

4. Create a daily time when family members can get together and share with each other how their day has gone. Encourage family members to really listen to what the other people say.

So then, putting away falsehood, let all of us speak the truth to our neighbors, for we are members of one another.

Ephesians 4:25

15

COLLABORATING AND SHARING IDEAS

We will work with each other, we will work side by side.

—from the song "They Will Know
We Are Christian By Our Love"

Collaboration means working with others cooperatively to accomplish common goals. People who do so together pool their skills and learn to give and take, negotiate and compromise. They support each other and affirm each other's strengths. To be in a collaborative relationship means to value other persons' contributions and see their role as enhancing what we do together. Developing working relationships with others results in living nonviolently because people experience the benefits of sharing.

We live in a world in which many people value competition more than cooperation. Often we find ourselves competing for jobs, for partners, for friends. We are encouraged to do our best and try to attain the goals we want. But a life without collaboration is lonely and difficult. To be an effective, nonviolent person, we must learn how to collaborate with others—sharing ideas, working with others, and combining talents to produce good outcomes.

The skill of collaboration can be taught to young children and requires many of the skills already presented here. In order to collaborate with another person, one must possess assertiveness, listening skills, an ability to give and receive feedback, and empathy. It involves blending the skills of others with one's own skills and requires a vision of the end product, a plan or strategy for achieving it, and a way of working together that includes compromise and negotiation, maximizing the gifts of each person participating.

My children have collaborated on school projects. Some of these group projects have required that they work with classmates to develop skits, reports, and presentations. Sometimes when they have worked with others, they have taken on a leadership role. At other times, they have played the follower. The leadership-follower roles can vary from time to time during the project.

Collaborators can demonstrate a level of humility as they give each other credit for the part each played. They acknowledge their own need for assistance, saying, "I could not have done this without you." They learn to be generous with feedback and support and do their best to help their collaborators.

Children have many opportunities for working together. They can collaborate in musical bands and orchestras, sports teams, Scouts, or spiritual youth groups. Many adults need collaboration skills on the job as they work on projects with others. In such situations, it is important to be able to draw the other person out, maximize their strengths, and combine the bits and pieces into a coherent whole project.

Some violent gangs do collaborate and work together to accomplish illegal goals, such as a robbery. So the ability to collaborate does not necessarily mean a person will be nonviolent. However, if the ends are positive, collaboration is an important skill to help people gain a sense of belonging and a sense of accomplishment.

Parents can teach their children to collaborate with others. Learning how to get along with those who are different requires sensitivity and tolerance. Questions parents can ask their children about working with others include

1. What kind of person do you think you work best with?
2. What are some behaviors that make a working relationship with someone else turn out the best?
3. How do you reject ideas from collaborators without putting them down?
4. How do you make your partner really hear what you are saying?

A Word to Children

You can work effectively with others to get things done. You can learn from them, and they can learn from you.

Moving into Action

1. Discuss the following with your children.

   a. What are some projects children and parents have worked on with someone else? What worked well? What didn't work?

   b. What are three ways you can help another person when you are working on a school project with them?

   c. What are three of your main strengths when you work with another person?

   d. What do you need to improve about yourself as you work with another person on a project?

   e. Who are some people you like to work with?

2. Create a collage together about what is important to your family using magazine pictures, words, scraps of material, stickers, and yarn. After you have completed it, discuss how you felt about working together.

Fools think their own way is right, but the wise listen to advice.

Proverbs 12:15

16

COMPROMISING AND NEGOTIATING

"You can't always get what you want."
—Song by Mick Jagger

V iolent people don't know how to compromise and negotiate because they lack the verbal and nonverbal skills to do so. When we live in relationships with others, we need to learn to get along. Conflicts will inevitably arise because our family, friends, and acquaintances want and need different things. As children go out into the world of school, they soon learn that others are different from them, have differing agendas, timetables, mindsets, attitudes, values, coping strategies, and belief systems.

The challenge of working, playing, and living with others involves learning to compromise and negotiate so that you get some of what you want and I get some of what I want. Negotiation is a way of asserting your needs and wants while taking into account my needs and wants. We negotiate to work out a solution that both of us can live with. We collaborate to bring about the best possible outcome. We mediate when we help others negotiate a reasonable solution in a conflict.

Conflict-resolution skills include

1. arranging an appropriate time to discuss the issue
2. clearly defining the problem
3. focusing on one issue; not getting sidetracked
4. being able to state your case clearly

5. using "I" messages as much as possible
6. listening with an open mind as the other person states his or her case
7. letting the other person know you understand what he or she is trying to say
8. demonstrating respect by reflecting back what he or she is saying
9. not judging the other person
10. brainstorming possible solutions that might work for both of you
11. being open to negotiation and compromise, coming up with possible alternatives, and demonstrating a willingness to be flexible
12. developing a plan of action
13. coming to an agreement with which you can both live
14. acting on your agreement
15. being a good sport and treating the other person fairly and with dignity

Although there are few opportunities for children to view healthy conflict resolution in the media, parents can use the media to teach negotiating skills. Movies often deal with explosive arguments, violent fights, or destructive ends to conflict situations. When you watch such a movie with your family, you can talk about all the other ways the characters could have resolved their conflicts peacefully.

There are many opportunities for children to negotiate and collaborate, and yet most schools still encourage children to work independently. In addition to teaching compromising and negotiating skills at home, parents can ask their children's teachers and principals to include activities and resources that teach about such skills.

Books such as *Families Caring* by James McGinnis and Mary Joan and Jerry Park offer the Peace Train for resolving family conflicts. When people disagree, they are asked to stop, identify the problem, generate solutions, check feelings that each member has regarding each solution, and negotiate a resolution. Another helpful book on the topic is *Fighting Fair for Families* by Fran Schmidt and Alice Friedman.

As with all the twenty-one nonviolence skills, you will teach your child most effectively when they see you practicing the skills, in this case negotiation, compromise, and mediation.

A Word to Children

Learning to negotiate and compromise means that you won't always get your way, but you will get along a lot better with others. You can learn a lot from them, too.

Moving into Action

1. A family vacation provides an opportunity to practice all of these skills. When the family is together for a week or more, certain decisions require compromise and negotiation. Where do we go? How much do we spend? What do we do? Who sits with whom? Who sleeps where? Do we stay together all day or split up. On your last family vacation, what worked well? What didn't go so well? If you had problems, why? What could you have done?

2. Parents, discuss this situation with your child: José wants to play soccer, but his brother, Manuel, wants to play checkers. How can they both get what they want?

3. Together watch a television program that involves a conflict (*The Wonder Years* is a good example) and come up with peaceful solutions other than the ones the characters came up with on the show.

*Do not use harmful words, but only helpful words, the
kind that build up and provide what is needed, so that
what you say will do good to those who hear you.*

Ephesians 4:29 TEV

17

CONTROLLING IMPULSES TO STRIKE OUT

The world we presently live in has chosen to ignore the message that patience is a virtue. We want things instantly, and if we don't get our own way, we have a tendency to flare up with anger. All too often that anger results in our own personal destruction and humiliation or the destruction of others.
—John Crudele and Dr. Richard Erickson

Human beings are capable of being impulsive or thoughtful, selfish or generous, rude or polite. We can say what is on our mind, or we can stop ourselves and consider whether saying it will benefit or hurt the situation. We can lash out physically, or we can control our anger and hostility and vent it in a nonviolent manner.

Most human beings are capable of thought, of analysis, of postponing gratification. However, many children do not learn to control their impulses. They watch adults who act, drive, or shop impulsively. They are bombarded with movies that show and reward impulsive and selfish behavior and include violent outbursts of temper and gunfire.

Often our first impulse is not always our best. We may have a tendency to demand what we want, have tantrums when we don't get it, and lash out at others. We may act in anger, in haste, and out of consideration only of ourselves. Instead of hitting or screaming when we feel frustrated or angry, we can leave the situation or go somewhere else to blow off steam. (Developing alternative ways of venting anger will be discussed in chapter 18 when considering how to demonstrate peacemaking, generosity, and concern for others.)

How do parents teach children to control their impulses to act and speak violently or foolishly? First of all, adults need to show their children that they can control their own impulses. When an adult demonstrates this, it can be brought to the child's attention. "See, I don't have to say the first thing that comes to my mind or do the first thing I think of."

Second, children need to learn how to stop in the midst of action. They can do this by learning to breathe or take a time-out. During this time, they can consider other options and choices and weigh the possible outcomes.

Third, during that time-out, they can use reason to come up with a response that might communicate their feelings and desires without inflicting pain on someone else.

Impulse control requires a level of maturity. A person needs to be able to reflect on his or her behavior and choose a course of action that will provide the ultimate best for all of those concerned. It means not always having one's own way and not always experiencing the immediate release that comes from venting anger. It means finding a safe and nonviolent alternative to express disappointment, frustration, or rage.

We can tell children, "Stop and think. Don't act. Don't speak. Ponder over your behavior and the potential you have to affect others—both positively and negatively. If you care about others and how they are going to be affected by your behavior, you will stop and reconsider whether or not to engage in that behavior. If you don't care about others, you will probably act without thinking."

If younger sister Juanita accidentally breaks one of Carlos's toys and apologizes, Carlos might respond by breaking one of hers, yelling at her, or hitting her. However, if he controls his impulse to retaliate, he can think about how bad she feels about it and how he could either fix or replace what has been broken.

When we act impulsively, we act without thinking. We don't consider our options, the consequences of our behavior, or how we affect others. Recently, an adolescent client from a good, upstanding family committed a burglary by going along with a group of friends. He was caught up in the excitement, and before he knew it, he broke into a refreshment stand and stole money. He was caught by the police and had to deal with court hearings and sentencing. When asked why he did it, he didn't really know. It was just what the guys were up to at that particular time; he went along without thinking twice about it.

Impulsive behavior can be positive, loving, and life-affirming. It can also be self-destructive and hurtful to others. Children need support, guidance, and tools to learn how to stop, take a time-out, and think before they act.

A Word to Children

Stopping to think before acting could save a lot of trouble and make your life better.

Moving into Action

1. Brainstorm with children both positive and negative impulsive behaviors. Examples might include driving without thinking about other drivers on the road, fighting back when you feel wronged, buying on impulse, and sending flowers to a friend. What makes some impulsive behavior acceptable and other impulsive behavior unacceptable?

2. Teach children different ways to stop themselves when they know they are acting impulsively in a negative

way. Do they take a deep breath, call a time-out, or leave the situation?

3. Joe exploded at Gretchen when she dropped her glass of milk on the floor. What are some other ways Joe could have expressed his feelings at that time? He could have made some "I" statements as suggested in chapter 14.

4. Parents, share with your children the times you have not said the first thing you thought or responded impulsively. Discuss how it was a wise decision and how you were glad you hesitated.

Get rid of all bitterness, passion, and anger. No more shouting or insults, no more hateful feelings of any sort. Instead be kind and tender-hearted to one another, and forgive one another, as God has forgiven you through Christ.

Ephesians 4:26 TEV

18

VENTING ANGER NONVIOLENTLY

Anger does not need to be a destructive or hurtful force. It does not have to trigger shame and guilt, destroy relationships, or create other negative emotional and physical consequences for us. Handled effectively, it can be a useful and energizing part of you, can build self-confidence, and can enhance your relationships with others.

—David Decker

Anger is an important part of our lives and a normal and natural emotion. It can be used to let us know our boundaries are being violated. It is often a sign that we feel some injustice has been done. It lets us know about our personal limits.

Violent individuals do not know how to vent their anger appropriately. They feel frustrated and powerless, hurt and overwhelmed, and it all comes out as anger. Many violent people do not allow themselves hurt, sadness, or fear, so everything erupts as rage.

David Decker, who has worked for many years in a treatment program for men who batter spouses, says that anger begins as a physical experience. "Anger is normal and natural emotion that arises from our interpretation of the 'fight or flight' arousal we all experience at times. It is a 'warning signal' that lets you know when something is going on around you that needs your attention."

Some people interpret events in a negative and blaming way and then become cynical and hostile. This cynicism and hostility leads to stress, and the stress builds to the boiling point. Finally, one last experience puts them over the edge, and they explode in rage—hurting themselves or someone else. Violent behaviors, according to Decker, are usually "an attempt to hurt, punish, intimidate or control others. They are a means of getting revenge or one's own way."

Certain words or behaviors often trigger anger. Known as anger cues, specific situations, people, events, places, times, or topics can cause a person to "lose it."

The first challenge for individuals is to watch for stress buildup and discover ways to relieve it. Time-outs, deep breaths, exercising, relaxation techniques, or changing the situation often help relieve stress. A person can learn some of these relaxation techniques from Decker's manual about treatment for violent men or from other books about stress relief.

The second challenge is to watch for those things that tend to unleash anger. People need to learn the specific cues that trigger their own rageful responses and try to desensitize themselves to those. How do you stop letting a cue bother you? You convince yourself that you won't be bothered by it. You tell yourself, "I am not going to let this cause me to lose my cool."

Decker believes that people need to take full responsibility for their own anger and not blame others for "causing them to lose it." Anger management involves finding safe places to vent and possibly yell and scream, punch pillows, and perhaps even cry. Built-up anger can be released if people get in touch with their pain, loss, sorrow, frustrations, and disappointments. Often anger is a cover for these areas of hurt.

Another way to cope with anger is to face the realities of life. Angry people often have unrealistic expectations of themselves and others. They may be perfectionistic and demanding. They might believe life ought to be smooth, even, and always pleasant. They frequently become indignant when they have to endure pain or disappointment. Teaching your child the complexity of life's journey and how we must accept the good with the bad is an important first step.

Allowing your child to experience the wide range of emotions and validating his or her feelings means that anger won't be the only allowable emotion to be felt or expressed. Sorrow, hurt, despair, loneliness, fear, and frustration can be vented in such nonviolent ways as talking, crying, or writing. Exercise is another way to deal with stress and cope with built-up anger. Children need good physical outlets to relieve the stress in their lives.

A Word to Children

Your anger can be your friend and tell you when you are being treated badly. Learning to release your anger nonviolently can help you get along better with others and still express your feelings.

Moving into Action

Discuss the following with your children. Share your own responses.

1. What makes you really mad?

2. When was the last time you were really angry? How did you handle it?

3. Brainstorm five nonviolent ways of venting anger.

4. What are some of the benefits of anger? How can anger teach you some things about yourself?

5. List five ways of venting anger that are hurtful and destructive to yourself or others.

6. Pretend that your friend Kevin has just hurt your feelings by saying some mean things about your mother. You are angry and wish to get back at him, but you don't want to do anything violent. What can you do to calm yourself down and create a nonviolent way to discuss your feelings with him?

If you become angry, do not let your anger lead you into sin, and do not stay angry all day.
Ephesians 4:26 TEV

19

NURTURING AND CARING FOR OTHERS

*There is a longing in every human being to be known,
to be deemed worthwhile. Without the possibility of
exchange, our very being as persons is threatened.
Life in solitude, if it persists, often has disintegrating
effects. . . . We die for lack of meaning, which is lack of
relationship. We need one another to know who we
are. . . . Jesus washed the feet of his own small community and bade them to wash one another's feet.*

—Joan Puls

Nurturing is a spiritual experience, seen by God as the way we need to relate to each other. It is the Golden Rule—to care for others as we ourselves wish to be cared for. Because most violent people lack interpersonal and empathy skills, they do not learn to nurture others. They often develop relationships with people who do not nurture them, and they may feel isolated even in the company of others.

We all need nurturing and support, and both boys and girls need nurturing skills—for most of them will be friends, lovers, partners, and parents some day. Nurturing others can be done verbally, physically, or spiritually. We nurture our friends by supporting them through their difficult times. We offer each other food, caring, time, and a listening ear. We cuddle, hold, and hug those we care about. We pray for those in need. Children thrive when they bond early with parents— through snuggling and cuddling, cooing and encouraging.

While we usually realize that babies and pets need to be nurtured, so do adults. Ashley Montagu in *Touching* claims that all human beings need affection and touch to sustain them in life.

Nurturing is the way to nourish friendships, to give of ourselves, and to show compassion and empathy. We nurture each other by offering small favors. We put ourselves out for the benefit of our friends and loved ones.

In the cold months of winter, my father would start up my mother's car before she went to work. Every morning, he would see to it that her car was out of the garage, running and warmed up by the time she needed to get into it. This was a sign to me, as a young child, that he genuinely cared about her well-being. It taught me how I could respond to my future wife. My mother, on the other hand, saw to it that my diabetic father's special food was always ready on time when he came in hungry from working on our farm.

Nurturing is best taught through example, but there are also direct ways we can get children involved in "doing" alongside us. Nurturing parents can talk to their children about why they nurture and can teach them how to do it effectively. We care for our elderly parents. We feed infants who can't feed themselves. We offer a backrub to our spouse who comes home from work exhausted and stressed. We take a pie to a new neighbor down the street. We send a card to a friend whose mother died. All of these are everyday examples of nurturing behavior.

We need nurturing especially during those difficult times of crisis, loss, and illness. However, we also need affection, support, attention, and care on a regular basis. Married couples need to model this behavior regularly so their children see adults who are loving, supportive, and compassionate. Children need to be praised and supported for being nurturing to their friends and family members.

A Word to Children

Think of how good it feels to have someone take care of you when you are sick or sad. You can care for others who need help.

Moving into Action

1. Take your children with you when you visit someone who is elderly or sick.

2. Invite some trusted stranger to a family meal during the holidays.

3. Think about those in your community who could use some care and nurturing. Write them a note, send a card, visit them, or send them flowers.

4. Within your family, make a conscious effort to do special and helping things for each other to show you care and to help make life easier for one another.

5. Remember a time when you were ill. Make a list of all the different ways people nurtured you.

Help carry one another's burdens, and in this way you will obey the law of Christ.
Galatians 6:2 TEV

20

SUPPORTING OTHERS THROUGH LOSSES AND DISAPPOINTMENTS

There are many ways to give. . . . Every time you extend yourself outward, the universe extends itself to you. Whenever you put another first, the universe puts you first. Strive to reach out and take the hand of the soul next to you. As you extend yourself in love, you will be uplifted to a new state of joyful awareness.

—Douglas Bloch

Caring for others creates a desire to help them when they go through hard times. Children who learn how to support others who experience a loss can help their friends make peace with those losses. My wife and I taught our children how to be supportive of their friends, whether when someone died or when a relationship broke up. We encouraged them to send a card, call on the phone, or just be there for their friends.

Being a comfort during other people's grief and disappointment is very important for mature development. If children have empathy and nurturing skills, they more likely will be supportive during someone else's losses.

Parents can help children learn how to help others during such times. Children over the age of six, for instance, are not too young to attend a funeral. However, they don't need to attend to be able to be supportive of a friend who has lost her mother, for example. They can be taught to say appropriate things to their friends.

"I am sorry about your mother's death."

"I will stand by you. Let me know if there is anything
you need."

"You can be sad around me."

"Sometimes people are angry when someone dies.
That's all right with me."

"You can talk to me about the person who died."

"I know this is hard for you now, but I believe you will
feel better in the future."

These are simple statements that provide reassurance and comfort to those who are grieving. Children also can be taught that their caring and presence matters more than any words they can say.

One reason to be supportive and caring during someone else's loss is that we might want them to care for us when we experience a loss. It is also a loving and mature thing to do. It helps others work through their pain and hurt and helps them move beyond anger. Chapter 4 deals with this in more detail.

Part of living in a community of caring means that we make ourselves available to others in need. This is our spiritual guideline, our primary commandment. Through supporting someone else in a time of loss, we learn to appreciate what we have. It can give us an incredible warm feeling to be of help to someone else who is hurting.

We also experience disappointments in life that are not exactly losses. We can be disheartened when we don't get a job or a promotion. We can be sad when our grades are lower than we expected. For many people, dreams don't always come true, and a person can be discouraged when he or she doesn't receive something they expected.

There are small disappointments and large disappointments. Noticing that people are disappointed means paying attention to the looks on their faces, how they stand or walk, or what they say. It then involves caring enough to say something to, do something for, or just be with those people.

A Word to Children

Being kind, being with people, and knowing what to say or do when they have gone through a hard time makes you an important friend.

Moving into Action

1. What are some losses you have experienced as a family? How have other people been there to support you?

2. Think of situations in which children or adults experience loss or disappointment. Brainstorm helpful things you can say to them.

3. Write a note, call, or e-mail someone who is going through a hard time.

4. Get the family together and think about all the ways you can help people in your community who are going through difficult times. Decide to do something together.

Let us give thanks to the God and Father of our Lord Jesus Christ, the merciful Father, the God from whom all help comes! He helps us in all our troubles, so that we are able to help others who have all kinds of troubles, using the same help that we ourselves have received from God.
2 Corinthians 1:3-4 TEV

21

LEARNING TO PLAY NONVIOLENTLY

It is possible to be competitive without having to be number one. Indeed, encouraging that balance between being motivated to compete and knowing oneself well enough to be satisfied with one's best efforts can make a person a more effective competitor. The balance of competitive spirit, high self-regard, and respect for others is a combination for a healthy personality. Our society does not glamorize this combination, but we need to help our kids develop this balance.

—David Walsh

As David Walsh says, sports competitiveness can be combined with respect for others. Through team sports, children can gain respect and many skills. Playing with vigor on a team can give a child a sense of accomplishment.

Play is a part of children's lives from their infancy. Girls typically don't seem to play as many violent games as boys, whose toys often come with guns attached. Boys are involved in more sports injuries than girls, and on the whole, they play rougher sports and play more roughly.

Some sports involve more violent and aggressive behavior than others. Baseball is less violent than football or hockey, for example. But even in a nonviolent sport, a violent confrontation can erupt. Media often focus more on the fights that break out during hockey games than on the games themselves.

Playing to win can result in ruthless aggression, taunting the other team's members, and intimidation. There are the "win at all costs" coaches as well as the coaches who want to teach cooperation and good sportsmanship.

Walsh points out that some team members are abusive to their own bodies during training. They overtrain and become injured off the playing field. Walsh says that "it has been estimated that more than a third of competitive youth runners will develop injuries from overtraining. Damage to shoulders and rotator cuffs from too much practice are the biggest problems for swimmers. Tendinitis and similar inflammations are a growing threat for young tennis and baseball players. And although pediatricians are raising concerns about these issues, 'playing hurt' is seen as a badge of courage in a society fixated on winning." Some athletes even use harmful steroids to give themselves a "winning edge."

Violence in play begins with action figures and war toys, includes aggressive blocking and intimidation, and ends with using cars as weapons of destruction. Aggressive, violent play takes its toll on human lives. How do we teach children to play nonviolently?

1. It is important to avoid toys of aggression and violence.
2. Check out coaches of soccer, baseball, hockey, and football teams before you sign your kids up to play. Some coaches are incredibly respectful and teach teamwork and good sportsmanship. Other coaches can be ruthless, arrogant, and aggressively demanding with your child.
3. Encourage learning the skills of a sport and being respectful of the other team.
4. Discourage negative cheering, booing, and hostile remarks.
5. Don't make winning too important. While you want your child to do well, the pressure to win all the time can be draining.

6. Encourage athletic activities that don't have winners and losers, such as jogging, strength training, biking, and other aerobic activities.
7. Value your child for his or her personality, generosity, and compassion, as well as his or her achievements in sports.
8. Point out healthy nonviolent athletic role models when you see them in the media.

A Word to Children

Respect for others is what good sportsmanship is about. Do your best and try to win fairly by the rules. Don't hurt anyone else, and try to keep from hurting yourself by overdoing it.

Moving into Action

1. Create a list of children's toys and games that are nonviolent and noncompetitive.

2. Brainstorm a list of the characteristics of a nonviolent coach. List the characteristics of a coach who is too interested in winning and who is willing to encourage violent behavior by his or her team members.

3. List the behaviors one would demonstrate in respecting the other team and in losing with dignity.

4. Discuss how parents encourage violence or excessive competition in sports. How might parents help to lower the level of aggressiveness?

Show a gentle attitude toward everyone.
Philippians 4:5 TEV

CONCLUSION: CREATING NONVIOLENT SPIRITUAL FAMILIES

To be human is to live in two worlds. Our posture, with our head raised to heaven, and our feet planted firmly on the earth, perfectly expresses our dual nature. . . . The human soul becomes impoverished when we try to escape the contradiction at the core of our nature. . . . The most powerful kind of spiritual practice, then, involves bringing these two sides of our nature together.

—John Welwood

Having read this book, you can begin to see that many of these nonviolent life skills have a spiritual component to them. By spirituality, we mean how we are connected to ourselves, to each other, and to our life source, which many people refer to as God. It has been said that every human being has a God-shaped vacuum in his or her heart—a special place that only God can fill.

The spiritually growing family is nonviolent and is committed to a set of principles that affirm life, encourage generosity, care for the community, and help members develop a sense of meaning and purpose. In order for this to occur, families must be intentional about their nonviolent spiritual growth. They require a place to focus their spirituality and a community to support it. Spirituality means seeing all of life as sacred and wanting to bring more love into the world.

One of the basic tenets of Christianity is the concept of grace, the belief in God's unconditional love and acceptance. This empowers all who believe in it to radiate that love to others. This love offers forgiveness when people admit their limitations and mistakes. It values all people regardless of their racial or economic backgrounds. It affirms that life is good, that we all have second chances, and that we are on a spiritual journey together. Many families believe in praying, singing, and worshiping together. Sharing their faith journeys, family members learn from each other and grow deeper in their understanding of God's unconditional love.

There is no one prescription for how every family might attain a sense of spiritual connectedness with one another. It does take work, commitment, intentionality, time, and effort. God intends for us to be whole, healed, and purposeful in our behavior. We are to grow, to care, to help unite the world, and to share our unique gifts with others. Healthy spirituality provides support, resilience, and a sense of identity.

A strong spiritual family is not overcome by despair when difficulties arise. They pray, trust God, and call upon their community for help and support. A strong spiritual family provides for others in need, knowing their own time of loss inevitably will come. They are not afraid to admit weakness and confess shortcomings, and they forgive one another and trust that hurts were not intentional.

Building nonviolent spiritual families requires a commitment on the part of the parents. They must share their own views of spirituality and agree on a basic framework. Parents develop ethical principles upon which they base their lives and live out those principles in front of their children. While they can try to influence their children, they cannot do their children's spiritual journeying for them. God has no grandchildren. Each person has to find his or her own way to be a child of God. But children learn a lot from their parents and the other role models they see daily.

Spiritually strong families are not aggressive, showy, or flashy. They don't run around trying to convert others. They live their lives with integrity, simplicity, and a sense of clear direction. They know their priorities, their purpose, and are intent upon healing the many kinds of suffering and disconnectedness that exist in the world. Such families read about faith and are willing to learn from inspired role models. They do not, however, blindly follow charismatic leaders who have found the "truth." Spiritually strong families are thoughtful and aren't afraid to question. They realize that faith grows stronger through questioning.

These spiritual families do not get caught up in current fads and fashions. They don't have to have designer clothing or make fashion statements. They know that what matters is God, God's love, purposeful and peaceful action, meaningful interaction, and trust in the process of life. They are cautious about the adults and children with whom their children spend much time. They want these people to be life-affirming and supportive rather than violent, aggressive, competitive, and shaming.

Spiritually focused families understand oppression and dedicate themselves to end it. They identify with the weak, the lonely, the outcasts. They work through peaceful means to bring an end to hatred, war, and violence all around the world. Spiritual communities can be of great help in providing support systems for raising nonviolent children. They can provide the biblical teachings and aid in the skill development so necessary for bringing about God's peaceable kingdom on earth.

A Word for Children

As you read the Bible, sing, pray, and celebrate with your family, remember that God loves you and the world and wants you to live in peace and to share that peace with others.

Moving into Action

1. In what ways do you understand God and Jesus as peacemakers?

2. How do you share God's grace with others? Do you forgive others as God has forgiven you?

3. How is your family committed to stopping the world's violence? What do you do, and what can you do? List the nonviolent spiritually related activities that you do as a family that bring about more peace in the world.

4. As a family spend some time each week praying for peace.

5. Create a peace prayer together as a family and share it with other families and friends.

May grace and peace be yours in abundance
1 Peter 1:2

BIBLIOGRAPHY

Personal and Interpersonal Skills

Beattie, Melody. "Boundaries Are Good." *Marriage Magazine.* March/April 1997.

Covey, Stephen. *Seven Habits of Highly Effective People.* New York: Simon & Schuster, 1989.

Crudele, John and Dr. Richard Erickson. *Making Sense of Adolescence.* Liguori, Mo.: Triumph Books, 1995.

Decker, David. "Anger: Your Enemy or Your Ally." *GentleMen's Network Newsletter.* 1997.

Erickson, Kenneth. Helping Your Children Feel Good About Themselves. Minneapolis: Augsburg, 1994.

Folkers, Gladys and Jeanne Englemann. *Taking Charge of My Mind and Body.* Minneapolis: Free Spirit Publishing, Inc., 1997.

Larson, Roland and Doris Larson. *I Need to Have You Know Me.* Minneapolis: Heartline Press, 1979.

McGinnis, James and Mary Joan and Jerry Park. *Families Caring.* St. Louis, Mo.: Parenting for Peace and Justice Network of the Institute of Peace and Justice, 1995.

Marone, Nicky. *How to Father a Successful Daughter.* New York: Fawcett Crest, 1988.

Thurston, Mark. *Paradox of Power.* Virginia Beach, Va.: A.R.E. Press, 1987.

Walsh, David. *Selling Out America's Children.* Minneapolis: Fairview Press, 1995.

Violence Prevention

Kivel, Paul. *Men's Work: How to Stop the Violence that Tears Our Lives Apart*. New York: Ballantine, 1992, 1997.

Miedzian, Myriam. *Boys Will Be Boys*. New York: Bantam Books, 1991.

Schaef, Anne Wilson. *When Society Becomes an Addict*. San Francisco: Harper & Row, 1987.

Schmidt, Fran and Alice Friedman. *Fighting Fair for Families*. Miami: Peace Education Foundation, 1989.

Sherrow, Victoria. *Violence and the Media: The Question of Cause and Effect*. Brookfield, Conn.: The Millbrook Press, 1996.

Wheeler, Joe L. *Remote Controlled: How TV Affects You and Your Family*. Hagerstown, Md.: Review and Herald Publishing Association, 1993.

Spirituality

Bloch, Douglas. *Words That Heal*. New York: Bantam, 1990.

Eittreim, Jean. *That Reminds Me*. Minneapolis: Augsburg, 1998.

Puls, Joan. *A Spirituality of Compassion*. Mystic, Conn.: Twenty-Third Publications, 1988.

Viorst, Judith. *Necessary Losses*. New York: Fawcett, 1987.

Welwood, John. *Love and Awakening*. New York: Harper Collins, 1996.

_____. *Ordinary Magic*. Boston, Mass.: Shambhala Publications, 1992.

Grief and Loss

Godfrey, Jan. *The Cherry Blossom Tree*. Minneapolis: Augsburg, 1996.

Huntley, Theresa. *Helping Children Grieve*. Minneapolis: Augsburg, 1991.

McNamara, Jill Westberg. *My Mom Is Dying*. Minneapolis: Augsburg, 1994.

Smith, Harold Ivan. *Grieving the Death of a Friend*. Minneapolis: Augsburg, 1996.

_____. *On Grieving the Death of a Father*. Minneapolis: Augsburg, 1994.

Strommen, Merton P. and A. Irene Strommen. *Five Cries of Grief*. Minneapolis: Augsburg, 1996.